Sowing Good Seed

TEACHING AGRICULTURE IN SCHOOLS:
THE SWAZILAND (ESWATINI) EXPERIENCE

By

Father David O.M. Gooday,
Prof. Comfort Mndebele,
Mr. Elson Khoza,
and Dr. Robert Langley-Smith.

2019

Sowing Good Seed -
Teaching Agriculture in Schools: The Swaziland (Eswatini) Experience
Context, Relevance and the Curriculum in a Developing Country
by
FATHER DAVID O.M. GOODAY, M. Phil. (Ed.), B.Sc. (Agric.), B.Th.,
PGC Ed (Exeter)

An Introduction and Chapter on Teacher Education
by
PROFESSOR COMFORT MNDEBELE
PhD (TVET); Cert. Adv. Grad Studies (TVET); MSc (Agric Educ.); MA (Educ.); BSc (Agric); Dip.(Agric)
Formerly Head of Department, Agricultural Education and Extension, UNESWA

A Description of Recent Developments in the Programme
by
MR. ELSON KHOZA, B.Sc.
The Current Senior Inspector,
Ministry of Education and Training, Swaziland (Eswatini)

Living Forward and Understanding Backward: How the Swaziland Experience Fits with Today's World: Challenges Associated with the Introduction of Agricultural Education in Schools
by
DR. ROBERT SMITH, M.B.E., M.A. (Ed), Ed. D. (Bristol)

ISBN: 9781796902440

Cover photo adapted from a photo by Visions of Domino

[CC BY 2.0 (https://creativecommons.org/licenses/by/2.0)]

For inquiries related to this book please contact Fr. David Gooday

Email: davidmalcolmgooday@gmail.com

Every effort has been made to make this book as complete and as accurate as possible, but no warranty of fitness is implied. The information is provided on an 'as is' basis. The authors and the publisher shall have neither liability nor responsibility to any person or entity with respect to any loss or damages arising from the information contained in this book.

ACKNOWLEDGMENTS

The authors wish to record their gratitude to those who have given them encouragement along the way, especially family, for their patience when we were writing. In particular, assistance from the following:

The Swaziland Agricultural Teachers' Association.

The Ministry of Education and Training, for permission to visit Schools and interview current teachers of Agriculture.

Respondents to surveys of former students.

We remember with gratitude those Government officials, headmasters, teachers, community leaders and others who supported the programme from the beginning with great enthusiasm.

Particular thanks are due to the specialists who volunteered to prepare the text books for the initial modules.

GLOSSARY AND ABBREVIATIONS

AEC	Agricultural Education Centre
AET	Agricultural Education and Training
ALP	Accelerated Learning Programme
DOMG	David Gooday, the author of this book
FAO	Food and Agriculture Organization of the United Nations
IIEP	International Institute of Educational Planning
IVS	International Voluntary Service
LDV	Light Delivery Vehicle (known locally as a 'bakkie')
MDG	Millennium Development Goals
MOD	Ministry of Overseas Development (UK)
MoE	Ministry of Education
ODA	Overseas Development Agency (UK)
PS	Principal Secretary
SACUC	Swaziland Agricultural College and University Centre
SAP	School Agriculture Panel
SAPP	School Agriculture Pilot Project
SAT	Schools Agriculture Trust
SATA	Swaziland Agricultural Teachers' Association
SDG	Sustainable Development Goals
SIDA	Swedish International Development Authority
SGS	School Garden Scheme
TETOC	Technical Education and Training Organization for Overseas Countries (UK)
TVET	Technical and Vocational Education and Training
UBLS	University of Botswana, Lesotho and Swaziland (to 1976)
UBS	University of Botswana and Swaziland (1976 to 1982)
UNESWA	University of Eswatini (from 2018)
UNISWA	University of Swaziland (from 1982)
UNDP	United Nations Development Programme
USAID	United States Agency for International Development

Table of Contents

PREFACE

This is not an academic paper. It is based on the thesis which Father David Gooday wrote and presented to the Institute of Education at London University, as well as Professor Comfort Mndebele's subsequent experience with training the teachers; and some inputs from the current (2018) Senior Inspector (Agriculture) in the Ministry of Education and Training, Mr. Elson Khoza, together with a number of individuals who had taken Modern Agriculture during the 1970s. Professor Bob Smith, who had a major role in curriculum development for the programme, provides an overview of the current status of agricultural teaching in schools in the developing world. We hope to show that it is a success story because those pupils who, while at school, underwent the training devised by the Schools Agriculture Panel, have benefited greatly from that experience. Whatever direction their careers may have taken, the youngsters who underwent the training which we devised have developed in many and various careers. Those boys and girls, now mature men and women, are approaching retirement and are able to look back on their working life in order to draw mature conclusions about their initial training. We have attempted to carry out surveys of former pupils of the programme, though effort to locate them through the Press and appeals to the SATA were of very limited success.

Modern Agriculture was introduced into the last three years of primary schools at the same time, but this book concentrates on the development in the junior secondary schools.

Many of the constraints in implementation of a project of this nature are well known. The emphasis in the Schools Agriculture Pilot Project (SAPP) was to identify these challenges and attempt to find solutions so that the maximum could be achieved to ensure that students learnt that farming, if properly practiced, could be a profitable, enjoyable and worthwhile activity.

FOREWORD

By Father David Gooday

I was working as a lecturer at the Swaziland[1] Agricultural College and University Centre (SACUC)[2] at Luyengo in the Middleveld of Swaziland in the late 1960s. Opposite the campus, was an Anglican church, the Usuthu Mission, which had been established late in the 19th century when the Swazi king allocated several hundred hectares of land to the Anglican Church. At one time the Usuthu Mission farm had been highly productive, and in fact it was the Director of the Mission who had introduced pineapples into Swaziland – where it is now an important export crop. When I went to visit the Mission, I found a few derelict citrus trees and not much else, but a large area of potentially arable land. I had a bright idea, and I consulted several friends about it – how about if we could establish a small training project for, say, 50 young school leavers, training them in basic production of the principal crops including maize, groundnuts, beans and vegetables, together with some information about raising livestock, and then after a few weeks, giving each of them an area of about two hectares, which they would run themselves, under the supervision of a trainer? After a suitable period – maybe a year, maybe less, they would go out and ask their local chief for a piece of land near their family where they could start to practice the skills they had learned.

I talked to Mike Armitage, an agronomist at the Malkerns Research Station nearby, and within 48 hours he had produced a series of maps with details of the soil types on the Usuthu Farm, land capability, and a suggested layout of what could be a training project. It looked very encouraging, and so I thought it was worthwhile consulting more widely. I was given the address of a very experienced consultant, Peter Batchelor of Rural Development Consultancy for Christian Churches in Africa, from Nigeria, and I invited him to visit Swaziland to give us some advice about which way to go. I was delighted when he accepted the invitation, but when he looked at our proposals he saw a number of difficulties and shortcomings. Probably the most important was that the success

---

[1] The name 'Swaziland' was changed by His Majesty King Mswati the Third early in 2018. In this book we are using the names as they were at the time (1970s) and use the changed name when referring to current issues.

[2] Now the Faculty of Agriculture of the University of Eswatini.

of such a scheme depended upon being sure to find land on which the trained youngsters could settle, and this depended very much upon the traditional system of land allocation, which was that chiefs usually allocate land to mature individuals and not to young school leavers! Problem number one! An equally devastating shortcoming was that our consultant believed that this sort of scheme was only likely to succeed where there was an especially dedicated leader who was able to introduce and continue to lead the project for several years to ensure a reasonable continuity. Such a person would be difficult to find, and furthermore the funding for a project of this nature would very likely not be obtained for a period in excess of three years at the outside! It was difficult to see how such a project could be made self-financing.

One day, while I was queuing at the Institute library, the man in front of me noticed that I was wearing a badge on my blazer which had 'SACUC Umhlaba Lifa' (which means: *The Soil is our Heritage)* on it. He asked me if I was from Swaziland. This turned out to be Bob Smith (co-author here!), who had just been recruited to join the University staff in Swaziland, and became one of my most helpful colleagues over the next few years. I love the word 'serendipitous' and this encounter certainly was!!

This visit took place in April 1971. Later in the year, I was due to take some sabbatical leave, and so I was able to travel to London, where I spent time at the Institute of Education trying to look into the whole question of teaching agriculture in schools in Africa. I will refer to what I found during my period at the Institute of Education in a later chapter[3]. After spending six months doing what is called 'desk research', I returned to Swaziland full of the idea that since we have schools all over the country, why don't we use these schools to provide the training which we had envisaged for our little school at Usuthu Mission? Surely we could achieve far more if we

---

[3] Chapter Two

taught agriculture in all the schools, as long as we set about it in the best possible way.

Having settled back at SACUC, I thought the best way of starting something would be to approach the Director of Education, in the Ministry of Education. So I made an appointment to see Mr. Leonard Sithebe to discuss my ideas. I was rather surprised and delighted to learn that the Government had already quite recently agreed on a policy to introduce 'practical subjects' into the primary and secondary curriculum. I remember clearly when Leonard said: 'I think I'd better introduce you to the Chairman of the Agriculture Panel'. He pulled a paper out of the drawer of his desk, and said 'Why, you are the Chairman of the Panel!' This was news to me, because I had only recently returned from London!

The result of this encounter was that Leonard set up a meeting including himself, the Educational Planner, representatives of the Economic Planning Office, the Ministries of Agriculture and Education, and the University. The minutes of that meeting show that '*It was agreed that Messrs. Sithebe and Gooday will liaise on the immediate activation of an Agriculture Panel in the Ministry of Education to make basic recommendations on the introduction of agriculture at primary and junior secondary levels.*' So this was the start! We had supportive Government policies and we had an official status as the Agriculture Panel of the Ministry of Education!! And we had enthusiastic support from the Ministry officials, notably from Mr. Sithebe himself, as well as the Principal Secretary and Minister of Education. But that was all – no finance, only one teacher, no equipment or buildings, no land actually allocated to agriculture!! Nevertheless – let's see what we can do!

INTRODUCTION

THE SCHOOLS AGRICULTURE PILOT PROJECT (SAPP)
by
Professor Comfort Mndebele

The Mission of Agricultural Education

The mission of agricultural education is to build awareness of and develop leadership for the food, fibre, and natural resource systems, articulating the vision of the future of agriculture, providing skills relevant to those entering practical farming, while recognizing the need for lifelong learning. In Swaziland, the teaching of agriculture in the secondary schools grew out of Agricultural Science in which emphasis was on "laboratory" sciences rather than practical farming. The Swaziland approach was to teach agriculture as a business, a practice and an applied science, placing emphasis on crop and livestock production. Fully conversant with the regrettable mentality of using agriculture as a menial activity, detested because of the attachment to punishment for misdemeanours in school, change of attitude was critical in the development of the goals of agricultural education. Hence the name change of the subject from "Agricultural Science" to "Modern Agriculture".

The Goals of Agricultural Education

Goal 1: Instruct in programmes about the food, fibre, and natural resources production systems. Evolving from primarily production, to the ever-changing science, business and technology of agriculture, entails regular changes in the content of instruction including agricultural science and technology, management of ecosystems to provide food and fibre, animal welfare, marketing, communications, public policy, environmental and natural resource management, food storage and processing, safety and nutrition, forestry, horticulture, landscape design and construction.

Goal 2: Serve all students equally, and equitably. The greatest resource for a productive agriculture and food system is people. Historically, agricultural education was attractive mainly to men resident in rural areas. However, it is now highly relevant to women, and must be relevant to all students entering entirely different fields.

Goal 3: Amplify the "whole person" concept of education, including leadership, personal, and people skills. Effective teaching and learning goes far beyond sharing information. The art of connecting formal instruction with application of information to real life situations makes learning relevant and stimulating. Individuals must have these "whole person" characteristics, which go beyond knowledge, to be successful in their pursuit of a career. Agricultural education provides this opportunity.

Goal 4: Develop educational programmes that continually and systematically respond to the marketplace. A common expectation of agricultural educators at all levels is to connect and work with the agricultural business and industry they serve. The benefits to students range from direct placement or partnership with business and industry for experiential learning. The teacher and the instructional programme benefit by having access to cutting edge agricultural technology currently used in business and industry.

Goal 5: Provide the stimuli that foster the spirit of free enterprise and develop creative entrepreneurship and innovation. A basic value of many involved in agriculture is the desire to own and operate a business. Agricultural education prepares students both for employment and for self-employment, and teachers are expected to foster the recognition of entrepreneurial opportunities and business ownership and operation.

Goal 6: Develop standards of excellence in classroom and laboratory instruction, and supervised enterprise experiences. Agriculture teachers need the ability to enhance the content and delivery by using three components: instruction, supervised agricultural enterprises, and agriculture investigatory projects. This sharing of ideas elevates the standards of excellence on which agricultural education is founded.

In short, the purpose of the Modern Agriculture programme is to produce capable, knowledgeable, contributing citizens. The Schools Agriculture Pilot Project was based on these principles, and this book describes how the programme was implemented.

CHAPTER ONE

Launching Agriculture into the School Curriculum

Education has many purposes, and educators will always enjoy debating the principal reasons why we have schools and universities, but very few will deny that one of the uppermost reasons why education is so important in the modern world is that it prepares boys and girls for life. Since very few of the pupils going into any school anywhere can be certain about the course of their lives right at the beginning, it is just as well to assume that some of them will become professionals in a wide range of fields such as medicine, accountancy, engineering, politics and who knows what else? An even larger number will be

> Through my education, I didn't just develop skills; I didn't just develop the ability to learn; but I developed confidence.
> **Michelle Obama**

involved in technical activities such as mechanics, building, plumbing, electronics, carpentry, welding, panel beating and other activities that make the world go round. Many more of them are likely to have to be content with running their own businesses, of whom most will have only a limited range of assets, probably largely their farms, livestock and perhaps a little machinery. These thoughts have some application universally, but more especially in developing countries. The only other assets they will have in many cases are the skills and attitudes which they have obtained during the first few years of their lives, partly from what they have learned from their parents and other members of the older generation, but especially from what they have learnt in school. It has to be admitted that in most countries – even in the so-called first world – insufficient emphasis has been placed on technical training, commonly called TVET, Technical and Vocational Education and Training. Is there anywhere in the world where there are enough trained and truly skilled plumbers, electricians, mechanics and other sorts of technicians? Is there any country where school leavers have adequate skills in basic farming competencies?

Importance of Life Skills and Livelihood Skills within the Curriculum

Surely therefore it is only sensible to ensure that the children have some idea about how to acquire the relevant skills such as mechanics, plumbers, bricklayers, housekeepers and – probably more in number than any other occupation – farmers. Of equally great importance is the acquisition and understanding of what we might call life skills - how to manage modern challenges such as dealing with the bureaucracy, understanding how institutions such as the law, the education system and the financial world work and a host of other issues. At another level pupils need to understand their role – the young person's role in society, in the family, in the nation, and many other life skills which are normally taught within the family. This is especially important where there has been a massive loss of the productive generation through the effects of HIV and AIDS, and the consequent death of those adults who would be passing on their accumulated wisdom and skills.[4] This constraint is of particular importance in Swaziland at the time of writing this book, although this was not fully recognized at the time when the planning of this project began in 1972.

Newsweek. November 2017
More than 130,000 job-seeking Poles have registered in Britain since the barriers came down. Polish teams now help to maintain the Channel Tunnel, Polish drivers are at the wheel of Britain's iconic double-deck buses. Polish workers, some recruited directly from Poland, staff the warehouses of leading supermarket chains. "I hear Polish everywhere I go," marvels 34-year-old Marlena from Katowice, who works in the London Underground.

Comment (DOMG). Yes, they are attracted by the money, but it is because there are so many jobs available in the UK – owing to the fact that there are **not enough technicians trained in the UK!!**

---

[4] Swaziland has one of the highest incidences of HIV infection in the world.

In trying to decide what is taught in schools, it is of the greatest importance that the programme (educators call this the curriculum) includes the basics for any of the possible career outcomes. There is always a debate about whether children should be divided into competency levels - the bright and the practical. This may be very unfair because some children are both bright and practically talented. There may be benefits of this grading at higher levels, but in the first few grades in primary and secondary school it is very questionable whether it is fair to the children. It is probably best to assume that all children are both bright intellectually and practically talented, and within a year or two skill levels will sort themselves out! So it is certainly necessary to include the most basic requirements – language and mathematics. The big questions are asked at the next level: What do the children need to learn?

In 1972, the Government of Swaziland decided that the subject of 'Agriculture' should be included as one of the topics to be studied, eventually, in all primary, secondary and high schools[5]. From the beginning, the subject was known as 'Modern Agriculture' to emphasize the scientific and commercial aspects. Introducing a new subject always creates problems because the teachers of all the other traditional subjects will start to complain about not having enough time to teach their subject – mathematics, history, geography, biology, physics, chemistry, language, religious knowledge and so on. As well as 'Agriculture' the Government had also decided that other practical subjects should be added to the curriculum – home economics (also called 'hospitality') and mechanical skills - although schools were given the option of selecting which skills they would include. But 'Agriculture' was eventually to be included in all schools for the very good reason that it was likely to be beneficial to all pupils, whether they became famers or entered agriculturally-related activities, or even went into the professions, since doctors and bankers often like to keep chickens or grow vegetables!

This book has been written mainly to show how a group of very dedicated individuals dealt with a whole series of challenges – most important of which were lack of funds and lack of trained teachers – to implement the policy which

---

[5] By 2018, this had very nearly been achieved, with the exception of a few urban schools with insufficient land available.

the Government had determined. It is hoped that these experiences will be of help to others faced with similar challenges.

The aims of this book

The main objectives of this book are:

To demonstrate that, given certain conditions, a successful programme of teaching Agriculture in schools can be developed and sustained, and that this programme is of long-term benefit to those who undergo it;

> The foundation of every state is the education of its youth.
> **Diogenes**

To identify principles and practices which may be adopted in a range of environments. The key principles which underlay the Swaziland Modern Agriculture innovation are well known but in this project they were brought together to address the shortcomings of previous international experience in agricultural education at the secondary school level in a culturally and environmentally appropriate model. This approach may serve as an example to agricultural educators and those responsible for development of school curricula mainly in the developing world certainly, but also in the so-called developed world, where this contention applies equally. Some of these principles are as follows:

The critical importance of an **appropriate government policy and supporting political will** to ensure a successful programme, together with individuals within the administration who are prepared to give the necessary support;

The **quality of the initial preparation** for introducing the programme;

The need for **key figures as champions** of the programme and the quality of programme leadership;

The development of a system of **implementation which will fit within existing structures** – such as related ministries and other bodies;

Development of a 'three legged pot' model in two senses: first, the involvement in the programme development of the Ministry of Education, the donor community and the beneficiaries (local communities, teachers, headmasters and, eventually, pupils and parents); and secondly to emphasize throughout the programme that Agriculture is essentially a practical, scientific and business activity.

The **emphasis on 'starting small'** by selecting a few schools; the Bridgehead rather than the Big Bang approach – to ensure manageability and relevance;

The eventual **institutionalization of the innovations** as the Ministry of Education takes over full responsibility for the programme from the initial team, by developing a supervisory and advisory structure of Inspectors.

Raising the threshold of abandonment – if at first you don't succeed, keep on trying! Also known as 'stickability!' It is essential that those responsible for implementation of the project are determined to overcome the inevitable problems they encounter.

Most of these principles apply equally to any curriculum development effort, not only to Agriculture as a school subject. The story which follows chapter by chapter traces the history of the Modern Agriculture innovation, drawing lessons from a specific intervention experienced over several years. This experience was subject to formative re-evaluation, reshaping and redirecting where necessary. This account of Modern Agriculture in Swaziland ends with a summary of the important factors which contributed to the success of the programme.

CHAPTER TWO

The African Experience of Schools Agriculture

It is generally very sensible, if one is starting off a new project in any field, to find out about the experience which people have had over the years. Formal education in Africa does not have a very long history if we are talking about schools and universities, although of course traditional forms of education have been known for many centuries or millennia. But the more formal type of education was brought in many cases by the missionaries coming mainly from the countries of Europe, particularly France, Belgium, Holland, Portugal and Britain (see box). Each of those countries, especially when, later on, the governments joined in the provision of education, developed its own style of education. More often, the missions had a primary objective of training possible future priests and pastors, while Governments, not always but mainly, were thinking of eventual replacement of expatriate civil servants with local individuals, a process eventually known as localization. (Little thought was given, during these early times, to the training of businessman,

> **OTHER COUNTRIES IN THE SCRAMBLE FOR AFRICA**
>
> Germany and Spain were also involved at one stage, and of course the United States was intimately concerned with the development of Liberia. Italy's involvement with 'opening up of Africa' was brief and concerned only with the north-west portion of the continent. Attention is drawn to the history of colonialism because its legacy was a disproportionate focus on academic rather than practical education, creating the 'habitus' or mindset still largely prevalent today.

professionals and administrators, other than civil servants!). Thus the type of education offered in those early years (say, from the mid-19th. Century on) had rather specific aims which were not much in line with the needs of countries which, during the middle of the 20th century, had emerged from colonization

15

with ever increasing populations and expanding economies. The provision of education for administrators and every aspect of society had to be hugely expanded to provide life preparation for all children, and to provide the necessary expertise for an expanding economy.

It is interesting and important to note that Bantu Education, which was provided for black pupils in the neighbouring South Africa, laid the foundations for the collapse of apartheid in that the shortage of skilled workers at all levels of business and industry led to the economic necessity of releasing Nelson Mandela, abandoning apartheid (separate development), and admitting black South Africans to the modern economy. Currently in that country there is considerable emphasis on skills development at the practical level, and this needs to include agricultural skills. It is important to recognize that blue collar skills are at least as important as white collar skills.

However, there were examples throughout Africa where efforts had been made to introduce Agriculture as part of the curriculum.

> The Prime Minister in Buganda said:
> '*We send our boys to the high school not to learn how to drive bullock wagons and to look after cows, but to learn to be fitted for posts of high standing.*'

For the purpose of this book, we are restricting this survey largely to the Anglophone countries of East, West and Southern Africa. Agricultural education in its broadest sense took place long before the arrival of any western influence. In most countries, instruction was given to girls by their mothers while boys learnt from their fathers how to carry out agricultural activities, largely by observation. Girls were involved with weeding, while in many countries, boys herded cattle from the age of about five. They learned by practical experience rather than through any formal instruction. In many countries, a system of apprenticeship was practiced within the indigenous tribal systems.

Formal education was introduced in the mid-19th Century, somewhat earlier in West Africa than in the East and the South. Farm schools were operating in Sierra Leone as early as 1847! But throughout the colonial period, the teaching of agriculture in schools was a highly controversial topic. Some schools in Uganda used to grow their own crops to help to finance the missionary-led education, while the curriculum remained largely academic. Some headmasters felt that instruction in agriculture was necessary for a 'well-rounded education' while there was much opposition to this view among indigenous chiefs (see box above) who were aware that the best English schools were mainly academic and so they demanded the same for their sons. This conflict of opinion was widespread through the continent. One of the reasons for this was undoubtedly because very often the 'school garden' became not so much a training facility as a source of vegetables for the teachers, and possibly income for the school!

The Phelps-Stokes Commission

A group of concerned eminent educationists, financed by the American Phelps-Stokes Fund in the early 1920s, were concerned 'to investigate the educational needs of the people in the light of the religious, social, hygienic and economic conditions, and to ascertain to what extent these needs were being met.' They noted that:

'it may seem surprising that educated natives have been opposed to any departure from the existing conventionalized school systems… Past experience has convinced some of the educated natives that the white man's methods have too frequently meant an inferior provision for the black people.'

The Phelps-Stokes Commission even suggested that Agriculture should be a core of the school curriculum. The (British) Director of Education in Tanzania in 1925, supported this view:

'As regards agriculture, it must, if a true perspective of our education needs is obtained, be made the basis of all education activity. If as the result of education a discontent with village life sets up permanent urban immigration, education will have failed. The school must not encourage the coming generation to despise the calling of its parents, but convince them that the cultivation of the soil is the most honourable of callings and that the future peace of Africa, first and last, lies in Agriculture.'

Support for this idea came from Jomo Kenyatta, a pre-eminent Kenyan leader, who later became President, who believed that *'Agricultural Education should be compulsory for Natives,* and that *'provision should be made for imparting technical training to Natives.'*

However, lack of funds became a dominant constraint at this point, due to the onset of the Depression (1930s) and also because Departments of Education very often did not possess the technical expertise to implement the changes proposed. Some confusion arose in East Africa in 1933 when it was decided that teachers of Agriculture should be controlled by Agriculture Departments, which stifled the implementation of Education Department policies. After the Second World War (1950s), R.J.M. Swynnerton, in Tanzania, observed that four fifths of middle school leavers would return to agriculture and that their education must therefore emphasize attitudes and skills required for self-employment. The policy of the Department of Education was that:

'the middle school course is designed to be complete in itself so that those who pass through it, whether they proceed further or not, will have received an education which will assist them to follow…whatever pursuits they take up…'

This touches on a most important point which is often brought up by those who have misgivings and doubts about a practical type of education. If the education is designed only for those – often by far the majority – who will continue on their farms in the rural areas, and not give the opportunity for those with academic and intellectual skills to progress elsewhere, then that education will be a serious failure and will be rejected by those forced to go through it. It would be compared with 'Bantu Education', the education offered in South Africa by the Apartheid regime, which specifically set out to deny the opportunity of further education for those who would have merited it[6].

Reasons for a lack of success in School Agriculture

While the teaching of agriculture in schools has often been regarded as unsuccessful, this has generally been based on the widespread misconception of the subject as a vocational one leading to employment in farming. If that was the objective, then it was not a success. However, at a farm school in Uganda,

---

[6] In 1953 the recommendations of the South African Eiselen Commission were passed into law, requiring separate systems of schooling for white, black, 'coloured' and Indian pupils. The provision for black pupils became known as 'Bantu Education' and was widely condemned as limiting in its aims, dramatically underfunded in comparison to 'white' education and wholly inferior in terms of its facilities and resources. It became a major ideological and political battleground in every sense.

the objective was *'to train young men and women to run progressive farms.'* Although only 15% of the output were in fact 'running progressive farms', 90% were employed in agricultural activities! The emphasis was on self-employment. Jon Moris has drawn attention to some of the underlying reasons why School Agriculture has so often been regarded as a failure. He wrote:

'The traditional view of Agriculture as being a terminal vocationally-orientated training was largely a consequence of the subject's amateur status. It had no clear rationale, no professional teachers, no instructional materials, no place in the examination system and no administrative supervision. As such it was bound to be a controversial and ambiguous part of the syllabus. A more accurate appreciation of its potentialities has awaited a time when it would be fully implemented as a bona fide subject of serious intellectual study'.

It paid dividends for those responsible for the programme described in this book to take note of Moris' warning.

Summary

In the few months before the School Agriculture Panel was formed, I had the good fortune of having been able to study the documents to which I have referred above (and many more) and so when we were faced with the challenge of putting together a programme which would effectively circumvent the problems, we had some idea of what we were facing, very much as outlined by Jon Moris in the previous paragraph. The deficiencies were: a lack of clear objectives; no clearly thought-out basic principles; very vague idea about the syllabus content at both primary and secondary levels; a lack of practically orientated textbooks and other teaching materials; a lack of adequate land and of suitable buildings and equipment. The programme had no place in the examination system; no attempt was made in many cases to make an evaluation of the success of what was being done; a lack of trained teachers; lack of supervisory personnel; a lack of coordination between the different levels of training (that is, primary, junior and senior secondary, and even with tertiary, which means either vocational or university level); a lack of publicity; and pre-eminently – a lack of financial and administrative support!

---

[7]   Moris, J.R. Farmer Training as a Strategy of Rural Development. Rural Development Report 28. Kampala. Faculty of Agriculture. Makerere University College.

We were, at least to a small extent, forewarned. What were we going to do to avoid the pitfalls and ensure that the School Agriculture Pilot Project (SAPP) got off to an effective start and really made a difference in the future lives of those who benefitted from this type of education? This is what we will discuss in the next few chapters.

CHAPTER THREE

Why Swaziland saw Schools Agriculture as an opportunity

Background Information

This chapter outlines the general situation in Swaziland at the beginning of the SAPP (1973). It will be of some help if we know something about the systems, influences and policies in Swaziland at that time, and it will help us to understand why the Government decided to introduce practical subjects, including Agriculture, into the school curriculum.

Swaziland has been independent

> On one Sunday, I was about to visit a teacher north of Pigg's Peak (in the north) when I received a request from another teacher beyond Nhlangano (in the south!). I was able to visit both, and be home for supper!

of the British since 1968, five years before the project started. The country is 17 364 square kilometers in size, making it the second smallest country in Africa[8]. This small size (about 180 km north to south and 120 km from east to west, about the size of Wales or New Jersey) was an immense advantage as it was possible to pay quick visits to schools for delivery of inputs, supervision of teachers and helping to deal with problems promptly, even if they were at the far end of the country!

The country is a neighbour to South Africa, which is much more developed and has a far larger economy. The 1976 census showed the population of Swaziland was just under 500 000[9]. That same census showed that at the time only 11.7% of the population was resident in urban areas, although the division between urban and rural is not at all well-defined.

---

[8] The Gambia is the smallest at 11 295 square kilometers, including the River Gambia.

[9] The estimated population of Swaziland in 2017 is 1.32 million and the median age is 20.6 years. This is an astonishing rate of growth of around 6% per annum.

An understanding of the system of land tenure, Swazi religion and other features, notably the political structure, is important in order to be able to judge the timing, content and method of curriculum development.

The royal genealogy goes back some thirty generations. In the late fifteenth century, groups of people who shared the Bantu languages migrated into south-eastern Africa. At some time in the seventeenth century, a man named Dlamini led a group across the mountains in the east of the country and became the founder of the Swazi royal clan in present day Swaziland. Since the early days, the mother of the ruler has had great influence on national matters. We often talk about the 'labadzala', the elders, of which the Queen Mother is the foremost and balances the power of the King himself. There is a duality of government with the elected parliament and modern style administration, being balanced by the influence of the traditional powers. The King's[10] authority is handed down to the approximately 120 chiefs around the country. Europeans, both British and Boer (now known as Afrikaners) arrived in the country during the 19th century and land, mining right and monopolies in various activities, were allocated to them by King Mbandzeni. By the end of the

century there was some confusion over ownership, and in 1902, the British assumed the role of protector. One third of the country was allocated to the 85 000 Swazis, while the remaining two thirds remained under the control of those who had been granted rights by King Mbandzeni. The ownership of land is now of two principal types: Swazi Nation Land (SNL) which is rather more than half, and Title Deed Land (TDL) with individual tenure. The

---

[10] The King, Mswati III, recently celebrated his 50th birthday as well as the 50th anniversary of Independence.

existence of these two types of tenure is very important as it affects Agriculture in many ways, and must be understood by teachers and learners who are studying Agriculture.

The climate is sub-tropical, and is also much influenced by the topography. The country is well watered, having five main perennial rivers flowing eastward and fed by numerous streams. This is very important for the present discussion, because it makes it possible for many schools to develop small irrigation schemes in the school garden. There are four main regions: Highveld, Middleveld, Lowveld and the Lubombo ridge in the east, bordering Mozambique, where the climate resembles the Middleveld. The Highveld is largely mountainous with deep valleys and steep slopes. Hail is fairly common and snow occurs every few years. The Middleveld has rolling grasslands, somewhat drier than the Highveld but still largely suitable for arable farming, though subject to occasional drought[11]. There are many areas with small irrigation schemes. The Lowveld is sub-humid and almost tropical but has been subject to severe drought in the last few years, especially in the south. The Lubombo is mainly used for small scale scattered dryland cultivation.

The small size of the country is important from several points of view. As mentioned above, all parts of the country are readily accessible, with very rare exceptions when there have been heavy rains. This facilitates ease of distribution of inputs such as seeds and fertilizers; marketing of produce at schools is somewhat easier even for rural schools; supervision of schools during the development of the SAPP[12] was immensely easier than it would have been in a country like Tanzania or Ghana with their far greater distances. Also the normally stable climate and good soils make it entirely possible for a competent farmer to make a fair living. There is a wide range of crops and livestock which can do well with good management.

Swaziland has a good communications network. The main roads are tarred, and many feeder roads are kept in reasonable condition by the Roads Department of the Government. There were at the time of writing two cellular telephone networks, which are rather expensive for consumers, but this

---

[11] From 2014 to the time of writing in 2018, there has been a serious drought with rainfall levels about half the long term average.

[12] Schools Agriculture Pilot Project from 1973 to 1979.

facilitates contact with teachers throughout the country for training and advisory purposes. But at the time of the SAPP this system had not been set up.

The Government's most important policy in relation to Agriculture is to assist Swazi farmers in making the transition from subsistence to semi-commercial and commercial farming. This support is carried out mainly through Rural Development Areas, of which there were four at the start of the SAPP. The main inputs are improvements in roads and bridges, soil conservation and irrigation development, improvement of cattle dipping facilities (to control disease-bearing ticks) and stock watering, domestic water supply, tractor hire services and many other improvements. The second aim is to encourage farmers on individual tenure farms; the third aim is to assist in the expansion of modern large-scale agriculture, of which sugar is the main crop. [13]

It is important to recognize that development is limited to four main core areas: the Mbabane-Manzini area, the Pigg's Peak-Bulembu[14] (Havelock) area, the North-eastern and the South-eastern Lowveld. The rest of the country, about 85% of the area with 75% of the population, is based on traditional agriculture, with a considerable gap in living standards between the developed and the traditional areas. Although this has changed somewhat in the last 45 years, it is still substantially the same as it was at the time when the SAPP started (1973).

Swazis live in family groups rather than villages. A man, with his wife or wives, children and a few relatives, constitute a homestead or Ekhaya. This scattered pattern of habitation increases problems of providing services such as schools, clinics, inputs and marketing facilities. Crucial agricultural operations such as weeding, are often carried out communally. Thus in Swazi society, there is a considerable tradition of cooperation. The absence of decision makers is often an important constraint on rural development. The man is usually the holder of the land, but often undertakes employment away from home[15] leaving the family to cultivate. The women are traditionally responsible for growing

---

[13] SWADE (Swaziland Water and Agricultural Development Enterprise) is an important agricultural development in the Lowveld and Middleveld.

[14] The asbestos mine at Havelock does not currently function.

[15] In the past, many Swazi men worked on the mines in South Africa. While this is still the case, numbers are now much reduced, around 4000 in 2017.

crops, but may be unable to make decisions concerning expenditure on inputs such as improved seeds or fertilizers or tractor hire.

Responsibility for agricultural education in schools lies with the Ministry of Education and Training. All pre-service training in agriculture (diplomas and degrees) is provided by the University of Swaziland (see box above). The Department of Establishment and Training and the Ministry of Local Administration

> At the time of the SAPP, Swaziland, together with Botswana and Lesotho, shared one university: The University of Botswana, Lesotho and Swaziland. This broke up in 1976 and the University of Swaziland was set up in 1982. Three other universities have now commenced operation: Limkokwing University of Creative Technology, the Swaziland Christian Medical University, and the Southern African Nazarene University.

have responsibilities for various aspects of agricultural education, the Ministry of Finance holds the purse strings, but the Economic Planning office is responsible for many decisions.

The education system is clearly defined. Primary schools provide a seven year course (Grades 1-2 and Standards 1-5). This is followed by three years of junior secondary and finally by two years of senior secondary in high schools. At the beginning of the SAPP, Agricultural Science was taught formally in only one high school, but in primary schools there was a School Gardens Scheme (SGS) which was supported by provision of tools, seeds and fertilizers. Teachers running this scheme had, for the most part, no formal training in agriculture[16].

The School System in 1973

Responsibility for agricultural education in schools lies with the Ministry of Education and Training, while all pre-service training in agriculture is the

---

[16] Despite this lack of training many primary teachers displayed considerable energy and talent in encouraging their students to develop very productive gardens.

responsibility of the university (UNISWA) which currently conducts three-year degree programmes for a range of disciplines within the Faculty of Agriculture and Consumer Sciences. This responsibility includes the training of teachers of agriculture although this was not the case at the time of the initiation of the SAPP. Most of the rural schools were not well equipped, having little more than classrooms and teachers and very little equipment. Many teachers were expatriates including teachers from South Africa, other African countries, and many volunteers from Europe, the United States and other countries, usually on two year assignments. The Government's contribution to educational finance was about 25% in 1973, the remainder coming from voluntary agencies, largely missions, and the parents. The introduction of Free Primary Education (FPE), commenced in 2017, and will change financial patterns substantially.

There were both primary and secondary curriculum units but neither of them had an officer with responsibility for development of an agricultural curriculum, and so coordination with these units was limited, though meetings did take place periodically. The structure of the Ministry of Education was straightforward and the position of the SAPP needs to be shown since there was no Senior Inspector for Agriculture. Of course, at this initial stage, the Senior Inspector (Agriculture) did not exist! This was the function of the writer who described himself as the Acting Unpaid Voluntary Senior Inspector for Agriculture.[17]

---

[17] The writer (Gooday) undertook this task at the request of the Minister of Education, Dr. Walter Dlamini, and with the permission of his immediate superior in the University, Mr. (later Professor) R.W. Bell.

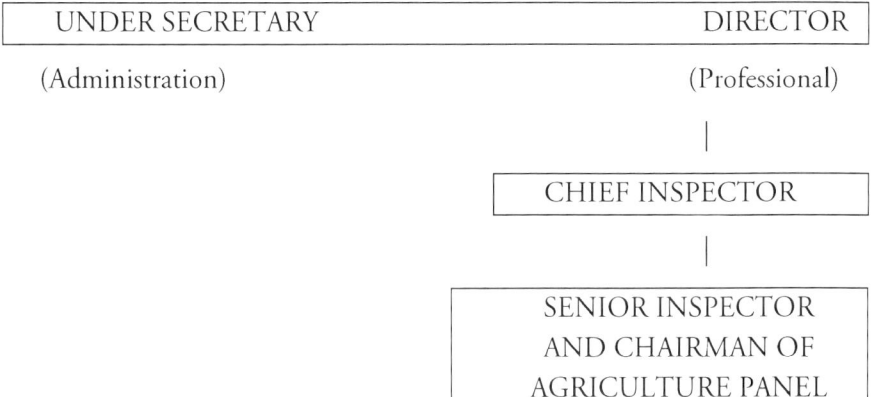

MINISTRY OF EDUCATION

| MINISTER |
| DEPUTY MINISTER |
| PRINCIPAL SECRETARY |

| UNDER SECRETARY | DIRECTOR |
| (Administration) | (Professional) |

CHIEF INSPECTOR

SENIOR INSPECTOR
AND CHAIRMAN OF
AGRICULTURE PANEL

<u>Recent changes</u>

During the 45 years since the SAPP was started, Swaziland (now named Eswatini) has changed considerably, notably in attitudes to development. With an increasingly literate population and substantial numbers of graduates and specialists in a wide range of professions, resistance to change has been much reduced. For example, the resistance to such simple improvements as fencing grazing lands has greatly decreased as people recognize the advantages of confining livestock[18]. This is symptomatic of the changing balance between the imprecision of traditional ways and the precision of modern methods, the vagueness regarding ownership, and the geometrical way of looking at things.

His Majesty King Mswati the Third, the King of Swaziland, recently introduced a strategy concerning the development of all aspects of Swaziland: He has stated that he expects Swaziland to have achieved 'First World Status' by 2022. Efforts have been made to define exactly what this means, but – even without definition – it provides a very clear guideline that every Swazi should strive to help the country to move forward in all aspects of life! Development

---

[18] Not the least of which is the release of boys from herding, making school attendance possible.

of the educational level of the population and of the level of agriculture are clearly very important aspects of this development.

The current Senior Inspector (Mr. Elson Khoza) has written a description of the developments in agriculture teaching in schools that have taken place in the years since the programme started (see Chapter 15 below).

CHAPTER FOUR

The Process of Introduction

Development of the School Agriculture Panel

The first meeting of the Panel was on 14th March 1972 and the initial members were:

A representative of the University (David Gooday, the writer, as Chairman);

A representative of the Ministry of Agriculture (Geoffrey Maina, the Director of Agriculture who proposed himself and supported the Panel with great enthusiasm);

A primary teacher (Mr. D. Dlomo);

A secondary teacher (Mr. K. Lapping);

An inspector of the Ministry of Education (Mr. J. Dlamini).

> Education is not preparation for life; education is life itself!
> **John Dewey**

A notable feature throughout the period of the project was the high degree of cooperation between the Ministries of Education and Agriculture. Sadly, too often in many countries there is an element of competition between these two ministries who are inclined to compete rather than to cooperate.

The outcome of this initial meeting was that:

'a pilot project in agricultural science be launched in a few carefully selected schools with a view to proving the value of agricultural science in the school curriculum, and then extending the scheme throughout the country.'

At the next meeting of the Panel on 2 June 1972, several important papers were presented including the following statement from the Director of Agriculture:

'education that denies, right from the beginning, the opportunity for a child to proceed to the top – without proving by examinations that he cannot – would easily be seen as the so-called Bantu Education … in a small country like Swaziland that is inevitably getting rapidly modernized, rural and urban ways of life are not splendidly isolated. The increasing improvement of communications and consequent services makes the rural and urban boundaries very blurred and artificial. Therefore

uniform types of education based only on the child's aptitudes should be the aim of educationists and educational planners.'

The Economic Planning office also produced a paper which outlined many of the basic issues which subsequently became the principles upon which the project was based. It was decided at this meeting that 'The School Agriculture Pilot Project (SAPP) should be initiated in January 1973 involving five primary and five secondary schools.

By the time of the second meeting of the Panel, there were only three months before the agreed date when the SAPP would be started –

> By this time, we had adopted the title 'Modern Agriculture' for the new subject, as opposed to 'Agricultural Science' or any other variation – 'Modern' gives a boost to interest, and new techniques and ideas would eventually improve the standard of farming in the country! Also, Agriculture is not only a science, but also a practice and very much a business and all three legs needed to be emphasized!
>
> **~DOMG**

January 1973! During these three months, we decided to adopt a 'package' (later called a 'modular') approach, and work was to be done on raising finance, selection of schools, identification and training of teachers, formulation of objectives, preparation of teaching materials, planning of buildings, equipment, irrigation and fencing requirements, and preliminary thinking about examinations and project evaluation.

Advantages in Swaziland

It is useful at this juncture to examine some of the advantages which we had in trying to initiate such a project in such a short time. First, Modern Agriculture was not taught in secondary schools and so there was no need to battle with pre-conceived ideas or vested interests. Secondly, there were no teachers of the new subject. This obviously appears to be – and was – a major problem, but it meant that the SAPP did not have to wrestle with in-built resistance. Thirdly, as mentioned above, the two ministries involved (Education and Agriculture) were on excellent terms. Fourthly, the country is small and it is quite possible to visit schools in the extreme north and south on the same day (see Box on page 19)! Fifthly, the hierarchy in the Ministry of Education was not very strict, and it enabled the writer, as an outsider from the University, to go directly to the Permanent Secretary, or even to the Minister, when decisions were required. Finally, and much the most important, Government policies, especially those of the Ministry of Education, indicated a genuine desire for the development of Agriculture in schools. This was clearly indicated by the Permanent Secretary for Education as follows:

'...we feel that the teaching of Modern Agriculture should be a part of the general education of everyone in the country and we hope that it will eventually be possible to introduce the subject at Standard Three in every primary school and at Form One in all the secondary schools.'

This effectively was a proposal for a six year course – the last three years of primary and the first three years of secondary schooling. Later on, the secondary programme was extended to cover Forms 4 and 5 – which is School Certificate level, but the secondary junior and senior programmes were distinct phases. Children in the earlier primary levels were regarded as generally too young to follow a syllabus in Agriculture, but would receive an introduction to nature study at a suitable level.

Summary of the Key Factors at the Outset

- New Government policy favoured teaching of agriculture in school;
- Individuals such as Leonard Sithebe, as well as the Principal Secretary and the Minister, were very enthusiastic and supportive;
- There was a good spirit of cooperation between ministries;
- The introduction of a new subject into the school curriculum did not cause a problem of overcrowding;
- Schools with adequate cultivable space were selected;
- The small size of the country greatly facilitated administration.

On the other hand lack of finance, teachers, supervisors and curriculum materials were challenges which needed immediate solution!

CHAPTER FIVE

Setting up the Structure: Aims and Principles for the New Programme.

Who is going to benefit from a programme of School Agriculture?

There are three principal groups who will be affected by a programme of school agriculture. First, there is the whole community, who even though they may not all be directly concerned with agriculture need to have an understanding of its importance in the economy of the country, the structure of the agricultural economy and its associated research, technical and advisory services, and some idea of the relationship between agriculture and other sectors of the economy. This group is particularly important in countries where Agriculture is both a major role player in the economy and also where the great majority of the population is involved in farming. Secondly there are those who are going to enter agriculture at the technical and technological level, the planners, thinkers, educators and executives in various agricultural services. Thirdly, there are those who will enter agriculture as farmers, either in the traditional sector as more or less subsistence farmers, or in the commercial sector. At any one time, an individual may be a member of more than one of these groups and he or she could belong to all three groups.

In the 'whole community' group, there are several sub-groups such as those with no schooling, those with less than four years of schooling and early leavers with sufficient education to establish literacy, but who have been unable to continue schooling for financial or other

> On one occasion, I took a group of recently arrived teachers for the SAPP to visit schools in the south of the country. We spent a while helping the established teacher to shell some green peas. The new arrivals had great difficulty in getting the shells to pop – they had never seen peas in pods before because, for them, peas came out of cans - these new arrivals were from a 'developed' country!
>
> **DOMG**

reasons[19]. The other 'whole community group' which needs special mention is 'girls and women.' The role of women in farming is of great importance, and this is often accentuated by the absence of men who have gone away for employment. In many countries, men give preference to their sons regarding educational opportunities. However, in Swaziland in 1973, the ratio was well balanced at primary level (51% boys to 49% girls), but at the secondary level the imbalance had crept in (56% boys to 44% girls). There are certainly aspects of the training programme which need to give special emphasis to girls, although it should be emphasized that the SAPP was aimed equally at boys and girls.

There are also sub-groups in the technical and technological categories. First there are advisers, extension workers, broadcasters, journalists, home economists and special advisers in crop or animal husbandry, cooperatives and other fields. Secondly there are research workers who are specialists conducting applied research to provide the extension group with the information they need. Thirdly, there is a group of planners and administrators. These are individuals involved in planning and decision making and in a small country, many of these decisions affect the rural sector so it is vital that those who move in this field are familiar with agriculture and its associated problems. This group can also include any worker whose activities affect the agricultural sector such as transport workers and those engaged in wholesale and retail marketing. The third group most obviously benefitting from being taught about agriculture in school is those who engage in farming, many of whom may have no other technical training other than what they learn in school.

It is difficult to determine the precise numbers in each of these categories, but in 1973, an estimated nearly 50 000 children had either received no education or had only a very short period in school, indicating a need for mass vocational education for the un-schooled. These included Rural Education Centres and Young Farmer Clubs. But for the bulk of the youth, an agricultural programme in school would probably be the only training in agriculture that they might receive.

---

[19] This group gives rise to what is known as the 'Primary School leaver problem.'

Aims of school agriculture.

A starting point in any consideration of the aims of teaching agriculture in schools is the policy of the Government. It is reasonable to accept that the aim of the educational system should support what was stated by the Prime Minister of Swaziland[20] in the Post-Independence Development Plan: '*a programme of socio-economic action, aimed primarily at improving the living conditions of the mass of the people.*' Sir Norman Alexander made the following remarks in relation to the University of Botswana, Lesotho and Swaziland[21], but they are very relevant:

'*The economists, sociologists and educators who have worked in this field regard education in two ways. In one, the aim of education would be the cultivation of the individual so that he may develop tastes, abilities and skills which will enrich his personal life in society; this is a consumer good. In the other way, education aims at training men and women in skills and techniques which will fit them to do work which will promote the economic growth and social development of their community; this is a producer good, and in this view of it, education is an investment which will maximize the economic use of all the resources .... Education must play three major roles: (1) provision of skilled manpower for the developing community; (2) generation of a mental climate favourable to growth and change; and (3) raising agricultural standards to produce a surplus for investment and at the same time a rising level of consumption within the community.*'

Jon Moris was mentioned above when he said 'the view of agriculture (in schools) as being a '*terminal vocationally-orientated training*' was largely a consequence of the subject's amateur status.' There is a range of opinions concerning what is the aim of teaching agriculture in schools. Some writers think that agricultural education in schools is primarily concerned with vocational training, and clearly, when the great majority of primary school leavers and increasing numbers of secondary school leavers will return to the rural areas, this aspect cannot be ignored. Other writers consider the question

---

[20] Prince Makhosini.

[21] The University of Botswana, Lesotho and Swaziland operated in all three of these countries, until 1976 when Lesotho withdrew from the partnership. After a period of university cooperation with Botswana, Swaziland established the University of Swaziland in 1982.

from the point of view of general education: the formation and development of the mind, and stimulation of attitudes conducive to change. Some aspects of the content of training need to give emphasis to the vocational aspect, regarding the training of technicians and of farmers, but even here the importance of attitude formation cannot be over-emphasized.

The Phelps-Stokes Commission makes a most important point: *'the first step towards agricultural instruction as an educational aim is a development of a real appreciation of its importance, covering the following topics: a realization of man's dependence on the soil; the importance of regularity, thoroughness and foresight; demonstration of the scientific elements of the soil and plant life; passing on information about the results of research; explaining the economic background and methods of marketing; emphasizing soil conservation and tree planting.'*

The World Conference on Agricultural Education and Training in 1970 considered that *'it is of vital importance that the image and prestige (see box on page 36) of agriculture be reestablished;'* and that one of the prime functions of agricultural education and training is *'the mobilization of the rural community for development, in particular among women.'*

Jon Moris[22] quotes ten principles for agricultural education put forward by President Julius Nyerere in Tanzania; it must: (1) create identification with the rural environment; (2) generate commitment to serving the rural community; (3) convey respect for existing rural achievements; (4) teach the fundamental principles of scientific agriculture; (5) give a sufficiency of essential skills; (6) develop the capacity to apply scientific expertise to local needs; (7) include practice in decision making; (8) teach the organizational patterns of modern farming; (9) make productive use of school resources; and (10) identify individual responsibility.

Field research on a variety of training programmes has suggested the following uses for School Agriculture within formal education.

- It is part of essential economic education in a country where most students eventually control agricultural investments in their own or relatives' farms – this includes virtually all non-urban wage earners and many urban dwellers as well

---

[22] Nyerere J.K. Education for Self-Reliance. Dar es Salaam. Government Printer. March 1967.

- It supplies a conceptual foundation for all subsequent adult education and agricultural extension so that rural students become at least minimally literate in a broad spectrum of agriculturally-related matters;

- It creates an awareness of career opportunities in many agriculturally-related fields which would otherwise lose the better students to the traditional occupations of medicine, law, theology and teaching;

- It measures aptitudes which are of great importance in national development: initiative, managerial skills, problem solving acumen, etc. thereby improving dramatically the selective ability of the examination system;

- It pre-eminently draws on local materials and institutions (in comparison with other sciences) which are readily available to all schools, and it relates directly to national development programmes within the school environs;

- It supplies the students and their families with reference materials (in the form of texts etc.) which apply immediately to the home enterprises, thereby deriving dual benefit from the effort of producing teaching materials;

- It can, if desired, inculcate proficiency in actual techniques of plant and animal husbandry. This vocational purpose is of most direct benefit to those who go on into technician's careers within a variety of agriculturally related fields, as well as those who enter practical farming.

PRESTIGE

The importance of prestige tends to be seriously under-estimated. Farmers need to be regarded as the most important citizens in any community because without them everyone would starve. A recent survey of the need for teachers in Africa estimated a need for around 50 million new teachers to cope with the huge increases in population, and the issue of **prestige** of the teachers was emphasized. The same applies to farmers – and hence the enormous importance and potential impact of agriculture as a school subject.

These quotations help us to recognize that there is a range of opinions from the idea that agricultural education is mainly a vocational subject suitable for teaching only at certain levels, to the view that it is, if well thought out, a respectable discipline having educational value in the broadest sense in addition to any vocational purpose which it may fulfil.

Analysis of the Role of Agricultural Education in Schools.

There is a unanimity expressed in the literature concerning the fundamental purposes of education which is in marked contrast to the working out of these aims. In considering these con-flicts, we have to answer a number of questions.

First, is education provided for urban or rural living? Clearly, in schools in urban areas, it is to be expected that the majority will continue to live in those areas. In rural areas a proportion will go to the towns to seek employment. In many countries of the South the 'drift to the town' is a major challenge. Although there has been considerable development of areas of Swaziland during the years since this project was implemented (over 40 years ago) it remains true to say there is still a very limited truly urban area (in the sense of a highly industrialized area), and the gradation from rural to urban is very gradual. The aims of agricultural education quoted from Moris above may therefore be said to be equally applicable throughout the school system

Secondly, when thinking of the vocational aspects of education, it is useful to remember that although the great majority will not reach the secondary level – though this will change over time – there will be a few who have a chance to go to the top educationally, since highly intelligent children may be found in every school. A balance in the curriculum between the needs of the child who will spend the remainder of his or her life as a farmer and of the other who will become an administrator, doctor or lawyer, has somehow to be found despite its inherent difficulty.

Thirdly, we have to consider the tricky question of quality versus quantity. Is it better to give some education to all, or to restrict it to a proportion of the population in order to ensure within the limited resources available, a certain proportion are educated to a higher level? Universal primary education has been introduced only in the last few years into Swaziland[23] and has probably been achieved without a major reduction in quality. Clearly, however the budget is limited and if it has to be spread over a larger number of schools and students, there is an inevitable risk of a reduction in quality.

Fourthly, there has to be a balance between designing the educational system to provide manpower for the economy and providing for the inclinations of individuals and communities. It was clearly the intention of the Scholarship Selection Board, when awarding scholarships that, as far as possible, the preferences of individuals would be followed[24]. A student wanting to become a doctor would be supported if he or she was well qualified, but the allocation of funds was clearly limited by the needs for different professionals. But this of course was at a much higher level in the system.

Fifthly, involvement in the community has been emphasized strongly by the fact that most schools have a school committee or a parent-teacher association, but the school itself needs to make an effort to get out into the community it serves, and the subject of Agriculture often gives many opportunities. For example, if a farmer is growing an unusual crop or keeping a particular breed of livestock, this is a great opportunity for a 'field visit'. The more that the school building is regarded as a community facility, the better.

Finally, it is important that whatever is good and useful in tradition should be retained. There may be contributions which parents can make in various aspects of the teaching. Certainly, there are ways in which the teaching of agriculture can involve mothers and fathers who may be especially talented in certain aspects of farming, such as a farmer who is very good at the construction of fencing; mothers who have special talents in food preparation, and many other ways in which parents can be involved. Secondly, pupils should know something about the traditional role of children in family or community affairs, such as boys herding cattle, and girls collecting water. These are acceptable activities, and pupils should understand that they have such responsibilities, making sure that these responsibilities do not interfere with school activities.

---

[23] That is, about 40 years after the SAPP was initiated.

[24] The writer was a member of the Scholarship Selection Board for some years.

Synthesis of the Objectives for Swaziland

The above discussion considers divergent views about the role of agricultural education in schools. There is undoubtedly a vocational function, but the learning of Agriculture in schools has a broader educational role. During the weeks prior to the implementation of the SAPP, the following was agreed:

The **overall objective** of the programme would be: *To encourage pupils (boys and girls) to regard farming as an enjoyable and profitable way of life when properly practised; and to stimulate positive attitudes to development and conservation.*

We said *'boys and girls'* in case anyone thought that the boys would do Agriculture while the girls did something else (like home economics*). 'Enjoyable'* was clearly important since one always studies far better if one is enjoying the studies. *'Profitable'* was also vitally important because in Swaziland it is possible to have a very successful business as a farmer. The mention of attitudes was also of the greatest importance because it is possible to become so keen on skills and book knowledge that the attitudes of students might be ignored.

We followed this with a brief description of what would be contained in the programme. The **approach** would include the following activities:

We shall:

- *teach practical farming, with an emphasis on underlying scientific principles;*
- *demonstrate and practice the business aspects of farming;*
- *provide a general knowledge of the dominant industry of Swaziland;*
- *provide a basis for future cooperation with the development agencies by promoting an understanding of their role and methods;*
- *create an awareness of career opportunities in farming and its associated technologies, and lay a foundation for further studies in agriculture.*

*The expected **outcome** of these objectives was that pupils would have:*

- *developed self-reliance, resourcefulness and problem-solving ability;*
- *adopted a scientific approach to modern farming;*
- *acquired practical agricultural and management skills; and*
- *gained an appreciation of the rural environment.*

We did not define exactly what would be taught and what would be the outcomes on each topic covered because these details would be provided in each of the teaching modules as they were developed. What was very important was to define principles of action so that all concerned (the Panel, headmasters, teachers, students and those writing the modules) would understand what we were doing and where we were going. These principles were as follows:

Local relevance. We would have to prepare our own set of teaching materials, and care would be taken to ensure that recommendations were compatible with local research and extension services.

Selective approach. It would be impossible in the teaching time available to cover a whole range of topics, so a selective approach would be adopted. This was always a problem because of the quite small time allocation. With a programme of 19 modules and time allocation varying from 6 periods[25] (Farm Records) to 33 (Crop Production), of which five were offered in the first year, eight in the second year, and six in the final year. Time allocation would relate to the relative importance of each module. In practice this initial allocation was far too heavily loaded and had to be pruned.

Time allocation in the timetable. This is the responsibility of headmasters and the Panel could only recommend. In practice, the advice was largely taken. Four periods per week in primary schools and six periods per week in secondary were considered a minimum allocation of time. The time allocated to each module should accord with agreed priorities and be based on the length of time each module required, practical modules needing more time. For example, Vegetable Production might require 25 double periods while Crop Storage might need 10 double periods as less practical time is needed.

Modular approach. Those topics selected for inclusion in the curriculum would form the basis of a series of teaching modules, each complete in itself but closely related to other modules intended to precede, parallel or follow the module concerned. Over time, the teaching materials to be prepared for each module would include a textbook, teachers' handbook, work cards and other visual aids, as well as the materials required to carry out practical activities.

Programming materials. Teachers should be provided with a comprehensive programme, including materials to be read to give guidance in teaching, practical demonstrations to be carried out and so on. The teachers' handbook

---

[25] Each of these figures for time allocation assumes that each class is 40 minutes, but Agriculture would be taught generally in double periods. 6 here, refers to six double periods devoted to Farm Records, normally covered in two or three weeks, or alternatively spread out over a period.

would describe how to conduct a class. Of course, more experienced teachers would be expected to have their own ideas on how to carry out their lessons. The handbook provided ideas about the lesson upon which the teacher could build but it should be sufficiently detailed to assist less experienced (or less energetic) teachers.

Teaching method. First, it should be assumed that pupils starting to learn Modern Agriculture may have a very limited knowledge of modern farming methods, and this should be borne in mind in presenting material. Secondly, sufficient time must be allocated to enable practical work to be done properly. Thirdly, the teacher should be prepared to guide the learning experience and provide resources, rather than to instruct. The catch phrase: '*show them how, tell them why, let them try*' is helpful.

Supply of materials. Most modules required materials in addition to books. For example, Vegetable Production needs adequate tools, irrigation, strong fencing, as well as seeds or seedlings, fertilizer and possibly spray chemicals (to be used very carefully, if at all).

Flexibility. Factors such as weather, the speed at which children learn and the competence of the teacher will determine the rate and order of sequence at which modules are tackled. The teacher should take account of these factors.

Class organization. Individual responsibility should be encouraged. Where this is not possible (possibly due to lack of space) the class should be divided into small groups – five has been found to be an effective size. On no account should class activities degenerate into an unstructured horde of children wandering about without guidance.

Integration. Every effort should be made to ensure that there is integration between the agricultural content of the curriculum and other subjects (especially science, mathematics and geography). But also (in secondary schools) how does the lesson relate to what was learnt in primary school?

Participation as wide as possible. The preparation (and evaluation) of modules should involve local technical experts, especially of the more experienced teachers. The first group knows what should be taught, and the second group knows how to do it!

Relationship to rural development. The teaching of agriculture in isolation can achieve little. It needs to be closely associated with a study of the comprehensive rural development of the country.

There were many other principles and decisions which arose as time went on including the following:

- Seven secondary[26] and five primary schools for the first phase;
- Preference to schools with a cooperative headmaster and a willing and able teacher, adequate space for field activities, and water.
- The list of schools selected by the SAPP would be approved by the Chief Education Officer;
- The selected schools would be supplied (as far as possible) with a teaching laboratory, garden materials as well as livestock buildings, fencing, irrigation and garden tools;
- Each module would consist of a pre-determined number of lessons;
- Limited vocabulary and straightforward grammar would be used;
- Agriculture would be presented as science, practice and business;
- Maximum participation of teachers in the curriculum development process (not possible right at the beginning due to lack of teachers!);
- The subject would be introduced at School Certificate level later, but as soon as possible.[27]
- Modern Agriculture would be compulsory in schools where offered;
- Only qualified teachers would be employed. This was very difficult initially because of the total lack of qualified teachers, but care was taken to ensure that the teachers understood the subject and were prepared to follow the guidelines.
- As far as possible, each module should contain practical as well as theoretical aspects.

Summary

In this chapter we have described the groups who may be affected by a school agriculture programme. We looked at the aims of school agriculture with

---

[26] This number was an increase from the originally agreed number of five because two schools were able to provide land, a teacher and many other facilities (tools, fencing, water, storage capacity) and were added to the five which would be provided with these facilities by the Panel.

[27] This was done several years later and is now an established part of the high school curriculum.

different views expressed. The SAPP debated many aspects of how to proceed and as a result a series of 'principles' were prepared. The next several chapters describe the main developments that were necessary in order to operate the programme effectively.

CHAPTER SIX

Getting down to the Detail: Financing the Innovation

The planning workshop took place in October 1972, and by January 1973 the SAPP was expected to start. Three working groups were set up and had a great deal of work to do to make sure that the programme would get off the ground in time. There were four areas where the work needed to be done: First, assembly of the necessary financial and material resources, including teaching

> Training is everything. The peach was once a bitter almond; a cauliflower is nothing but a cabbage with a college education!
> **Mark Twain**

materials and practical facilities needed to carry out the programme. Secondly, selection of schools at a very early stage so that the necessary practical facilities could be assured in good time. Thirdly, provision of the necessary human resources: teachers, and staff for supervision and distribution roles. Fourthly, the system of examination had to be developed. The teachers would be provided with a considerable amount of assistance in conducting the programme, but they needed to know about the examination which the students were expected to aim at. It was also necessary to let the public know what was being developed, and keeping all relevant bodies informed. Each of these aspects will be dealt with in the following chapters.

The first and most important pressing issue was that of finance. Where were the funds going to come from? When the Agriculture Panel was first established, we were not aware of any funds available anywhere to get the project started! Many observers regarded it as quite impossible to start the programme in any schools in the time available. It was the fundamental issue, because without funding we could not develop curriculum materials, recruit teachers or develop practical facilities at the schools. The Ministry of Finance officer indicated that the possibility of raising sufficient finance from the Government or a donor was 'remote!' However, his advice was that if the Panel could implement the project in the first year or two in order to demonstrate that there was a serious intention to establish an effective programme, then the prospect of finance becoming available on a substantial scale was good. Estimates were prepared based initially on three assumptions: first, that there would only be five secondary schools, whose selection would be determined partly on the grounds that existing irrigation facilities would be adequate; tools would be supplied to these schools by UNICEF through the existing School Gardens Scheme; and E2 500[28] (yes, two thousand five hundred emalangeni!!) would be available from the budget of the Ministry of Education. In fact, seven schools were started as planned in January 1973. One of these was Salesian High School, which obtained E3000 from the US Embassy. At a later stage, two more schools (Edwaleni and Ebenezer) were brought in because they had competent (though not agriculturally trained) teachers. Tools were supplied by the School Gardens Scheme to five of the schools, and the Ministry funds were made available! The cost estimates for the first year were very meagre. The following figures represent the initial estimates and are per school:

CAPITAL COST		RECURRENT	
Tools	400	Seed	10
Fencing	50	Fertilizer	30
Water distribution (cans)	200	Chemicals	5
Shade house	100	Lab equipment	50
Store	750	Protective clothing	20
Total	1,500	Total	115
Total capital and recurrent: = 1615			
Cost for five schools = 8075			

The first year cost, including E5 500 for primary schools, was E13 575. Several organizations were approached with a request to help bridge the gap. After the schools had been selected, a revised estimate was produced. Two of the schools produced most of the funds required, and the revised total figure was E9829. In December 1972, the US Embassy donated E7500 to match funds from the Government and donors. On 10 December, it was finally

---

[28] This figure equated with a year's salary for a university lecturer in 1971

decided to proceed with the SAPP and the initial curriculum work had to be completed by January 1973

Efforts to locate funds for the second year continued. A letter from the Secretary of the Group Chairman's Fund of Anglo American illustrates the attitude of several potential donors:

'...although we are interested, and could consider an appeal in principle, it will probably have to be along the lines that you would have to get the project started without our help and that we would consider coming in at a later stage.'

The British High Commission went so far as to express misgivings over the likelihood of British finance for the SAPP due to their prior experience with school agriculture.

So what the potential donors were saying was *'get on with it and see what you do, and then we will see if we can help you!'*

In May 1974, a cheque was received from Anglo-American to make up for the estimated shortfall in the budget for the second year. It was decided by the Panel at this stage that an account should be opened for donations to be deposited and this is how the Schools Agriculture Panel Fund was established[29]. In subsequent years, considerable financial assistance was received from numerous sources. Between 1974 and 1976 a total of nearly E61000 was received and was used chiefly

Donors included Anglo-American Corporation of South Africa; Bread for the World; Christian Aid; Mennonite Central Committee; Miserior; Oxfam; Save the Children Fund; Shell; Tear Fund; US Embassy; Carnegie; UNICEF; Usuthu Pulp; Swaziland United Transport and one other source donated materials.

for purchase of a vehicle, production and printing of textbooks and salary for the curriculum development specialist who was employed at a later stage but for whom no Government post existed. It was assumed that the initial group of

---

[29] This developed into the Schools Agriculture Trust of Swaziland Revolving Fund which has been dormant since 1986.

schools would proceed to Year Two of the curriculum and that a further five primary and five secondary schools would start the programme.

In 1974, a detailed budget was presented to the Ministry of Finance with estimates up to 1979, based on the experience of the initial year. It was assumed that a further seven secondary schools would start an Agriculture programme each year. These proposals were submitted to the British Overseas Development Agency (ODA), which must have had a change of heart, since the proposals were accepted. In March 1975, an officer was appointed as Senior Inspector for Agriculture[30]. By 1978, 20 secondary schools were offering an Agriculture programme.

At the same time as these developments were taking place, the University of Swaziland was developing a Diploma in Agricultural Education designed to overcome the shortage of teachers and dependence on foreign teachers. This Diploma was started in 1977 and will be discussed in a future chapter.

Summary

First, a very considerable sum of money was spent, though not of course in the first year. Much of this was of a capital nature and the facilities developed are likely to be used over a period of many years. It is not feasible to produce accurate costs of the whole scheme because many figures were hypothetical and administrative costs of Government are difficult to assess. However, although the exact number of pupils in participating schools is not known, if a conservative estimate of 40 students per class and two classes per school are used, this gives a minimum of 7440 pupil-years over the four year period and an expenditure if E71.44 per pupil year.

Secondly, the existence of a private source of funds raised from voluntary agencies had a very important effect. It enabled the SAPP to be started when Government funds were inadequate, and to be continued for two years at a scale well above that which would have been possible if only Government funds had been available. Despite lack of funding from Government, the SAPP was always considered as an entirely Government programme. This outside source of funds enabled a four year period for the development of the textbooks. Once these books had been developed and refined, it became feasible to approach

---

[30] This was Mr. Chris Teale.

commercial publishers (Oxford University Press) to take over production. It enabled the system of coordinators, later called inspectors, (described below) to be developed through the provision of a fleet of five vehicles including a lorry. Vehicles were kept on the road at crucial times when the need for repairs might otherwise have brought support services to a standstill. Secretarial services were hired, labour employed and incidental costs covered such as payment of railage charges without which unacceptable delays would have occurred. A number of schools obtained their own private finances for particular projects such as the development of a larger garden, a dairy unit and a beef enterprise.

A further point was reached when it was no longer possible to provide free textbooks, as had been achieved in the early stages. In 1977 and 1978 they were published by Oxford University Press and sold through the Schools Agriculture Panel Fund at cost. This point is important for two reasons. First, the books had reached a point of development when they were sufficiently professional to be worth buying. Secondly, it was possible to order several thousand copies, and to operate a revolving fund which collected money from schools and paid the publishers. This enabled costs to be kept far lower than if books had been sold through commercial booksellers, and it also ensured that every school obtained the appropriate books in the required numbers. However, administrative functions to keep this system going were considerable, and in 1979, sales were handled through a commercial bookshop.

Another use to which private funds were put was in the operation of a revolving fund for the purchase of seed, fertilizers, lime and chemicals. As with the books this enabled the Panel to ensure that every school, without exception, obtained the recommended varieties of seed and fertilizer in suitable quantities at minimum prices and at the time when they were required. Regrettably, as the number of schools increased, the administration of this system became burdensome and had to be discontinued. These products are available through cooperatives, and schools now purchase their requirements through cooperative or commercial sources.

Finally, the policy regarding financial independence in each school had to be examined. In each school, initially, the Form 1, 2 and 3 programme recurrent costs were financed mainly by the Panel for the first time they were operated[31]. Thereafter, schools were instructed to become self-financing. Recurrent funds were held by the Schools Agriculture Panel Fund which could be used in emergency, such as the outbreak of poultry or rabbit disease, hail storms or other incidents, but schools were recommended to charge an agricultural fee of One Lilangeni (E1) for each pupil in Form One, Form Two and Form Three. This would serve three functions. The first function was that it enabled the Agriculture Teacher to purchase the inputs he or she required at the beginning of each year. The funds collected in the first year were in theory to be put on one side so as to form a float. If costs increased, schools were expected to raise the agricultural fee to a level which would cover costs of inputs for the year.

The second function of the Agricultural Fee was that it could be related to the teaching programme and could be used to teach about input-output relationships. It was recommended that pupils should pay the fee which, at least notionally, would cover input costs[32]; then at the end of the module, they would record the mass and value of the produce and either sell it or take it home. It was expected that the value of produce would greatly exceed the amount of the Fee. The third function of this approach was that it gave teachers an incentive to organize the productive modules in such a way that they would be profitable. In practice, schools varied in the policies they adopted. Some schools did not charge an Agricultural Fee as such, but obtained such financial support as they needed from general school funds. This system satisfied the need for funds to purchase inputs but it did not satisfy the need for pupils to learn about input-output relationships since pupils did not see the School Fee as covering agricultural costs if it were not specifically stated to be for that purpose. It did satisfy the incentive to be productive provided that the headmaster did not subsidize the programme out of school funds. Another variation adopted in some schools was that they did not allow pupils to keep the produce or money raised from the sale of produce. In these schools, produce was sold and the

---

[31] This was the case for vegetable and crop production costs. The main inputs for Poultry and Animal Production (chickens and rabbits) were provided directly by the Panel at no cost to the school.

[32] For example, in Unit Two Vegetable Production, it would cover the costs of seed, fertilizer, chemicals, notional rent of the land and hire of tools.

money kept in the Agriculture Fund to be used for improvements as perceived necessary by the Agriculture Teacher; or in some cases it was used for some collective class activity such as hire of a bus for a class visit to some place of agricultural interest. In one case, the headmaster insisted on handling all financial matters himself. The result of this was a breakdown in the financing of the project at this school. The possibility of misappropriation was such that Agriculture Teachers were requested to be responsible for the handling of agricultural funds; they were to keep proper accounts and they were to be submitted for regular audit by the Coordinator[33] (now known as Inspector) for that school.

A discussion of the financing of school agriculture would be incomplete if it did not draw attention to a weakness often experienced in the past. Too many schools have opened up a piece of land, planted a single crop and sold the produce to bring money for the school. This money earning potential of agriculture is no bad thing and the Tanzanian programme of self-reliance strongly emphasizes agricultural projects operated largely by the staff and students of the schools. The danger lies in the very great risk that this objective may be regarded as the most important, and this has often been the case in the past leading to a reduced emphasis on the longer-term learning and attitude development aspects of such programmes.

This description and analysis highlights the complexity of financial issues underlying a school agriculture programme. Sufficient finance is essential, and these issues must be considered in detail before and while the other important matters of materials, teachers, supervision and examinations are being developed.

---

[33] See below for a description of the functions of a Coordinator.

CHAPTER SEVEN

Developing Teaching Materials

Once a decision had been made to proceed with the SAPP after the initial financial constraints had been at least partially overcome, particularly by the substantial support from the US Embassy, it remained for the principles underlying the development of a curriculum to be put into practice. This chapter deals with the following items: development of the syllabus; textbook; teachers' handbooks;

> The expression 'teaching materials' is usually used to cover books, teacher's guides, posters and other visual aids, but in teaching agriculture, other aids which are essential include the practical facilities for livestock and crop activities. See Chapter 8.

workbooks, work cards; reference books and visual aids.

The syllabus

In December 1972, SAPP did not proceed immediately with the preparation of a syllabus. However, in 1972, an initial outline of the modules to be developed had been prepared; the writer of each module was requested to prepare detailed objectives for that module and to present them in a format which would go forward to constitute a section of the syllabus. In this way, the detailed preparation of the syllabus followed the preparation of the textbooks. The reasoning behind this was that if a syllabus, which is essentially a summary of material to be covered, was to be prepared, this could be done far better after the details of each lesson and each textbook chapter had been thought out. Thus the syllabus actually prepared represented a summary of all the topics covered in all the modules. Although the syllabus was important, the detailed material in the textbooks and teachers' handbooks was much more important as the basis for the syllabus.

Pupil's Textbooks

The principles of textbook development had been evolved, and general topics of the modules had been defined in detail with time allocation for Form One, and in summary for Forms Two and Three. The writer prepared Module One: 'Plants and Man' as an introductory module and this was duplicated and circulated to the writers of Modules Two (Vegetable Production) and Three (Plant Growth and Environment) who had been recruited and were all volunteers! It was designed to help

One of the remarkable features of the School Agriculture Pilot Project (SAPP) was the extent to which '**volunteers**' carried out so many of the activities. Some of the volunteers might describe themselves as having been **cajoled** rather than volunteered but there was an immense amount of goodwill for the project!!

children find out what plants are cultivated, and to explain the value of the plants they have discovered to man and animals. By the middle of January, Modules One, Two and Three had been typed illustrated and duplicated. The writer also developed a teachers' handbook, a workbook for students, and work cards for each module (described below). The textbook, workbook and teachers' handbooks were all prepared on A4 format paper. These materials were ready by the middle of January for a two week training course for the agriculture teachers. Modules Four and Five were ready by the end of the second school term and all these materials were distributed to the schools by the writer in his own car.

Further modules were prepared for the new school year by January 1974. Additional modules awaited the arrival of the Curriculum Writer in July 1974. Thereafter, the remainder of the Form Two and Form Three modules were steadily produced from July 1974 until February 1976 by which time all the modules had been produced in their original format.[34]

---

[34] There was a delay with Module Six – Crops in Swaziland. It was intended to use film strips to illustrate various crops because the range of climatic conditions in the country prevented some crops being raised in some schools (such as citrus and sugar)

Each module was produced in a different colour. In the second year, minor alterations and corrections were introduced. In the third year of production (i.e. 1975 for Form One) the

> It is what you read when you don't have to that determines what you will be when you can't help it.
> **Oscar Wilde**

books were printed by offset litho, paid for with funds from the School Agriculture Trust referred to above plus donations from several agencies. This made it possible to distribute books to all students free for these initial years. In subsequent years, the printing of textbooks was taken over by Oxford University Press who have been responsible for the production of all subsequent editions over the following forty years.

Teachers' handbooks.

The teachers' handbooks were essentially designed as an aid to the teacher in lesson preparation. Apart from a few technical notes, therefore, they were concerned with method rather than content. As a consequence of this, nearly all the handbooks were prepared by the editors rather than the writers of the modules. There was no participation from teachers in preparation of these initial handbooks because at this early stage, there was only one agriculture teacher and he lived far away from where the preparation was being undertaken. Later on, once there were many teachers, they were able to participate in the improvement of the various teacher aids, and their criticism was of great help.

As the teachers' handbooks were prepared, a number of desirable aims in the structuring of lessons became apparent such as a clear statement of the objectives of each module, the overall time allocation recommended, a list of materials required and ideas to ensure that a variety of activities would be undertaken. Finally, further explanation of technical points could be given where necessary.

In Phase One the handbooks were presented separately. In Phase Two, handbooks for Modules Two and Three were printed but this proved to be uneconomic and all subsequent handbooks were duplicated, the numbers required per annum being less than 100. From 1976, the handbooks for all modules in one year were bound together in one booklet for ease of reference.

Students' Workbook.

In the first two years of the SAPP a workbook was distributed to be used with the matching textbook. The workbooks were A4 format and consisted of questions, diagrams and charts to be completed, blank diaries to be filled in and so on. The chief purpose was to encourage the students to express themselves in writing; inculcate habits of accurate financial and physical record-keeping; stimulate reflection on activities in which students had participated; and on occasion to develop artistic talent. However, the cost of producing a workbook and distributing it to a rapidly increasing number of students was prohibitive. As the materials development moved from Phase One to Phase Two a change in policy was adopted. All the questions and former workbook activities were listed at the end of the related chapter in the textbook. Where charts, graphs or other diagrams had been given they were replaced by instructions on how these might be prepared. Students were to purchase an exercise book such as might be used for any other subject. This exercise book would serve as a workbook for all the modules in one year. There were two other reasons for discontinuing workbooks. They did not prove sufficiently durable when subjected to the rigours of the classroom; and secondly, their production and distribution constituted a major logistical problem.

Work Cards.

The other category of written teaching materials prepared was the Work Cards. Two types of Work Card were developed. A series of 14 informational Work Cards was prepared in which material was presented on a series of topics including environment, pollution, and other important issues. This type of card was discontinued after the first year because of the difficulties of revision which it created for the pupils. If this information was suitable for inclusion in the programme, then it should be in the textbook itself.

The second type of card was instructional. These cards were related to practical activities and set out in detail how each practical activity was to be carried out. For the first year only, all cards were painted with lacquer as a protective measure and the intention was that they should be used in the garden or elsewhere outside the classroom, or for laboratory activities, and thus the soiling of textbooks would be averted. After the first year, no attempt was made to lacquer the cards for the sole reason that the task was too massive to be undertaken with the labour resources available. These instructional or Activity Cards were of two types,

The initial teaching materials were produced in a decidedly 'garden shed' way. The materials team had drafted ideas including the information to be presented, any examples to be used and the kind of simple illustrations to accompany the unit or module. This was all done on a Gestetner stencil which was then used to run off the dozens of copies needed for distribution to schools. Often the materials to be produced were needed on an emergency basis. The team's usual illustrator of modules remembers the support team arriving at his office early in the morning with stencils in hand asking if the blank spaces could quickly be filled with a sketch of a hen-house, or a maize crib! Once done the stencil was rushed off for printing and the materials delivered to the schools.

group cards and individual cards: Each school was provided with a suitably sized wooden box to keep the cards safely and conveniently.

These Work Cards were continued until the end of the Pilot Project (1976) but were then discontinued for two reasons: first, the number of cards to be produced for new schools and as replacements for lost or damaged cards in old schools had by this time become very substantial. The number required in 1977, assuming 50% replacement for old schools, would have been 22 560! Also the cost of production would have been considerable since the cards cost over two cents each. The logistical problems were better avoided and the cost of production had become excessive. Secondly, it turned out that in practice the teachers made very little use of the cards because, they said, the time consumed in distributing and collecting the cards was time wasted. The teachers found that

ABILITY TO FOLLOW WRITTEN INSTRUCTIONS. This deficiency among many of the pupils indicated a severe lack of ability to read and put into practice what they had read. This was a criticism of the quality of primary education where students needed to learn how to read, mark, learn, inwardly digest and put into practice!!

the pupils were often unable to follow even quite simple practical instructions on the cards without verbal explanation[35] (see the box above). Very often, the teachers would want to carry out a variation of the activity so that the cards would confuse rather than help.

A third type of card was contemplated, but never produced, mainly owing to pressure of time. This would have been a Supplementary Card. In many of the lessons outlined in the handbooks, pupils were expected to work as individuals and at their own speed. It was to be expected therefore that some pupils in a class would finish the set work before others. It would have been useful to provide schools with a set of cards of supplementary activities, such as finding a reference in one of the resource books with which each school was provided.

It is important to mention that throughout the SAPP and beyond, a system of colour coding was used in order to facilitate the use of the materials. In Phase One Year One for each module the textbook, handbook, workbook and work cards were produced in the same colour so that the relevant materials could be found more easily. In Phase One, Year Two, an economy was achieved by making the first page only of the correct colour. The reason for this is that coloured paper is more expensive than plain white paper.

---

[35] The ability of students being taught in a second or third language to comprehend written material in a metropolitan language has been widely researched; the findings have always been disappointing, even at the tertiary level.

Resource books.

In each year of the SAPP, a small number of Resource Books and periodical subscriptions were provided to each school. The objective was to provide each teacher with a range of books on the topics covered by the modules. Lists of recommended books were obtained from Kenya, Zimbabwe, Tanzania and Uganda and a list of recommended books was prepared and distributed to teachers and to students of Agricultural Education at the Faculty of Agriculture. The

> You can only learn so much from books. You can only learn so much from education. Ultimately, it is the wisdom of God that will carry you through in the toughest situations of life.
> **Ravi Zacharias**
> (or common sense! DOMG).

headings in the list were crops, livestock, land use and mechanization, agricultural economics and agricultural education. There were four categories: required, desirable, suitable for library, specialist.

Visual Aids.

The last category of teaching materials to be discussed is visual aids. It was recognized that all sorts of aids like pictures, models and samples are very helpful as teaching aids. Due to a lack of personnel in preparing the SAPP, very little was achieved in acquisition or preparation of visual aids. This was seen as largely a function of the teachers themselves. Some teachers produced a range of charts and posters which were used to illustrate lessons and appeared to be very effective. At a later stage, a Visual Aids specialist was recruited and among other items he prepared a series of film strips relating to the modules. This was important, because the very varied conditions of the schools throughout the country resulted in certain crops only being grown in certain areas (eg sugar in Lowveld and Middleveld, but not in the Highveld).

CHAPTER EIGHT

Practical Facilities

All the materials so far discussed have been written or illustrative. Even more important in the development of the SAPP was the provision of a full range of practical facilities. This chapter deals with the provision of land and buildings; equipment for the laboratory, garden and workshop; irrigation; fencing and expendable materials. The appropriate provision of all these

> The most valuable achievement of all education is the ability to make yourself do the thing you have to do, when it has to be done, whether you like it or not
> **Aldous Huxley**

resources ranks with the quality of teaching and learning materials, the efficiency of supervision and support and the creation of a 'facilitating environment' at the systemic and local levels as critical factors in programme success.

Land

The availability of an adequate area of land with soil of good quality is a fundamental requirement for a school agriculture programme. Quite a wide range of opinions existed concerning how large a plot was required, from a farm (any size!) to a much smaller area. In Tanzania, 2,4 hectares (6 acres) was considered sufficient; others thought that as little as 0,8 hectares (2 acres) was adequate for a class. Another view was that four square metres per pupil was sufficient. In Swaziland, the area of the garden was determined first by the number of streams[36] in the school. The second factor was class size, and it was assumed that class size would not exceed, but might reach, fifty. The third determining factor was to consider the area required for each of the practical modules requiring land (notably Vegetable Production, Crop Production,

---

[36] By 'streams' in this context is meant the number of separate classes in a given school year; such classes might be organised by perceived ability of the pupils or on a less formal basis.

Forestry and Fish Farming). Allowance needed to be made for livestock facilities, water storage (a dam), crop storage facilities and so on. A realistic calculation indicated that half a hectare (1.25 acres) would be a bare minimum requirement for each school.

Soil samples had to be taken when a potential site was being considered, and a soil agronomist visited each site to classify the soil and pronounce it suitable for vegetables and crops.

Education is that whole system of human training within **and without** the school house walls which molds and develops men and women.
W.E.B. Du Bois

Buildings

Over the period of the SAPP, a laboratory/workshop/store, poultry house and rabbitry were built for each school. Each of these developed from a simple building for the first group of schools to more complex buildings in subsequent years, The initial concept of the laboratory/workshop/store was as a 'potting shed', in which tools would be stored in one lockable portion, and an area large enough for a class would be used mainly for construction, repair and demonstration activities but also for simple laboratory activities such as germination tests. Also local builders were employed by the Panel for the initial group of schools, and schools were requested to supply labour and to supervise the builder. This approach was attractive to donors, but proved unsuccessful in a number of respects. Of the nineteen SAPP schools, four (of which three were mission schools) were able to build the workshop themselves to a plan provided by the Panel, and produced satisfactory buildings. A further reason for the lack of success is that the design was considered inadequate but was gradually improved over time. The result of these improvements was that the initial cost of E1800 rose to E7000, partly due to cost escalation. There were, at the basis of this transformation, two opposing philosophies, both important. On the one hand, the simpler the building, the more it would resemble those found in surrounding areas; for the purpose it had to perform, a simple cheap construction was entirely adequate. On the other hand, two influences were brought to bear: first, the building was in practice often used as a classroom, even though this should not have been necessary since every class had its own room. Teachers explained that the reason for this was that they preferred to conduct classes in the Agriculture building because all the equipment was readily available if it should at any time be required during a class. Secondly, the building was compared with other school buildings, such as the classrooms and particularly the science laboratory, and there was considered to be a very unfavourable comparison with regard to construction and appearance. This was thought to give Agriculture a bad image. Another pertinent consideration was the siting of the building. In schools where it was immediately adjacent to the classrooms it compared unfavourably. In schools where the garden was a distance from the school (750 metres was considered to be the maximum acceptable distance); this comparison was irrelevant since the building was identified with the garden rather than with the school. In some other countries, such as Tanzania and Kenya, much more complex and lavish buildings have been constructed for the teaching of Agriculture. The debate continues!

The poultry houses constructed for the first Form Two classes were of five metres by five metres dimension with gum-pole uprights interspersed with a block wall one metre high. This was divided into two portions, the smaller portion sub-divided into four sections, each large enough for eight deep litter laying hens. In the larger portion four sets of battery cages were suspended. Thus there was room for sixty-four birds in batches of eight. This was sufficient for eight groups of pupils, with five or six per group. Each school was provided with houses according to the number of streams in that school. Some teachers thought that this method of construction was too lavish in comparison with local methods of poultry keeping.

In the subsequent year, a similar house, but slightly larger, was constructed as a rabbitry, and rabbit cages were supplied to accommodate two batches of eight cages. It was decided that only a rabbitry would be provided for the Animal Production module, but any schools wanting to keep another form of livestock would be free to do so and over time pigs, beef and dairy cattle were kept in some schools.

In 1976, the fourth year of the SAPP, all these houses were replaced by one block-built house with blocks spaced for ventilation, and room for two batches of poultry and one batch of rabbits. This became necessary because the original structures were too susceptible to theft. This improvement became possible when more funds were available.

Fencing

The construction of fencing for each school garden was necessitated by the widespread incidence of 'trespass' by uncontrolled poultry, goats and cattle as well as human predators. For each school, the length of fencing required was measured, and gum poles, barbed wire and wire netting were provided. One of the first duties that each teacher was required to do was to construct the fence around the school garden. There were very few problems with fencing and teachers and pupils were strongly encouraged to be sure to close gates at all times.

Schools were encouraged to use more traditional methods of fencing when necessary and possible. This could be done with brush wood and any other solid material. Even better was the idea of planting appropriate plants along the fence to develop an impenetrable hedge.

Irrigation

The presence of water not too far distant from a school was one of the factors determining school selection. The approach to solving the problems of irrigation varied widely from school to school. Sixteen schools had water pumped from a nearby stream. In the case of five of them, the supply was inadequate and the Panel had to purchase an engine and pump and have them installed by irrigation specialists. In one school, water was drawn from the town water supply; in one school there was a derelict dam which was repaired; finally, one school had an excellent gravity fed water supply.

Once an adequate supply to the garden was assured, two further developments were necessary. First, one or two 9000 litre (2000 gallon) tanks were installed as a reservoir, since the demand for water actually during a class was invariably greater than the rate of supply. This reservoir enabled a class of fifty pupils to draw water for vegetable plots without exhausting the supply. Secondly, a system of piped reticulation throughout the garden supplying a minimum of six taps was installed, again with the purpose of minimizing delays in watering.

One school developed a fish pond of five by ten metres in size. The clay bottom was puddled by the pupils to render it watertight, and a platform was erected from which pupils could fill their watering cans.

Despite these provisions, numerous problems arose with water supply. Once installed, pumps were the responsibility of the schools, and if they failed, the Public Works Department of the Ministry of Power, Communications and Works was called upon to repair them. There were often long delays, sometimes for months. In some cases, the Coordinator was called and was able to bring spare parts, tools and expertise, but in many cases, the problem was protracted.

Livestock

The provision of livestock was an important responsibility of the Panel. There were two species provided: poultry for Module Eight in Form Two, and rabbits for Module Fourteen in Form Three. In 1974, birds were provided in February at five weeks of age. The advantage of providing young birds was that pupils were involved in rearing them to point of lay, but the grave disadvantage was that they reached point of lay in June when schools were closed. Schools were recommended to sell the birds at the end of the school year in order to avoid caring for them during the long Christmas vacation, but this resulted in the birds being kept for a period of only five months. Laying birds are most profitable if kept for about eleven months, so this project design was unsatisfactory. In 1976, the hatchery in Swaziland was prepared to raise birds up to point of lay so that the birds could be distributed in February which allowed a nine month laying season, and the project became more profitable. Some schools decided to keep the birds through the long vacation at Christmas in order to increase the profitability, but these were large schools with support staff.

Schools were expected to purchase the required feeds, but where this was not possible, feeds were delivered by the Panel.

> Without education, your children can never really meet the challenges they will face. So it's very important to give children education and explain that they should play a role for their country.
> **Nelson Mandela**

The necessary ancillary equipment, including drinkers, feeding troughs and egg trays, were supplied by the Panel.

In February 1975, the first group of schools was supplied with rabbits, three does and a buck. Feed was supplied, as with poultry. Some schools had problems with marketing the rabbit meat since rabbits as a domestic animal are not common in Swaziland[37]. Some schools managed to establish markets for rabbit meat in nearby towns, but the scope was limited, so schools kept the number of does down to three or four. Bucks were interchanged between schools periodically to avoid in-breeding. The reason for supplying rabbits was that they were mammals, similar in that respect to cattle, sheep and goats, so that principles could be taught such as nutrition, cleanliness, health, disease control and so on. It was not practicable in any other than the very large schools to consider using larger animals as the ideal for learning principles due mainly to difficulties of cost, distribution of inputs, marketing and so on.

Garden and workshop tools

A major area of expenditure was on provision of garden and workshop tools. The policy was that the major garden tools would be provided on the basis of one between two pupils, and other tools in appropriate numbers. A simple range of workshop tools and a bench with a vice was provided for repair and simple construction. Schools were expected to maintain the number of tools required. In addition, a small range of laboratory equipment was provided including test tubes, beakers and flasks and some other items required to carry out experiments.

Expendables

Some inputs were required on a regular basis. These included agricultural lime, fertilizers, seeds, some garden chemicals and feeds for the livestock. These were supplied by the SAPP coordinator on his or her visits. Where schools were able to purchase their requirements in local towns, this was preferred and was aimed at as an eventual method of supply, but for the initial period, assistance in providing these supplies was needed. This was financed by the Panel during

---

[37] Rabbits are popular for meat among Mozambiquans. Several teachers and former students have taken up rabbit production as a small enterprise.

this initial period, but some schools proved to be slow payers, and so a policy was adopted that no school which had failed to pay for inputs in January/February (Vegetables) would be supplied in July with the requisites for Crop Production. This proved effective. Quantities required by each school were calculated by the Coordinator. The range of fertilizers and seeds was kept to a minimum to avoid complications.

Because of the range of equipment and materials supplied to each school, each teacher was issued with a clip file and a set of stock cards, one card being used for each category of equipment and recording the number received. Teachers also had to sign a Government Stores 'Issue and Receipt Voucher' for whatever tools or input materials were delivered.

As can be imagined, the provision of physical facilities and equipment became a major aspect of SAPP over its lifetime. Beginning, as noted, with deliveries in the writer's own car and developing into a fleet of vehicles and coordinators, the maintenance of supplies and equipment became a critical dimension of the programme and one which cannot be under-funded in any similar innovation.

CHAPTER NINE

Teacher Development

The success of any rural development project in terms of the extent to which its objectives are achieved, both in education and in any other aspect of bringing about change, depends very largely on the quality and dedication of the personnel involved in its implementation. Quality, in the context of an agricultural education programme, is taken to refer to a number of attributes the most important of which are technical competence and knowledge of all relevant aspects of agriculture, professional competence as a teacher and teacher motivation. By this last is meant a willingness to work long and hard with dedication to the achievement of the

> Education is the key to success in life, and teachers make a lasting impact in the lives of their students.
> **Solomon Ortiz**
>
> The giving of love is an education in itself.
> **Eleanor Roosevelt**

programme objectives. In addition, an important quality is the ability to inspire efforts in others. In the case of the teachers this means the pupils, and for the supervisors, the ability to inspire the teachers; and finally, an ability to persevere with a job until it is finished, and if something does not succeed, to try again and again until it does succeed. This quality is possibly the most important of all because in an innovative programme of the nature of SAPP there are bound to be – and certainly were – many difficulties and challenges which often require great determination if they are to be overcome! There is a need to raise the **threshold of abandonment** – don't give up!!

This chapter examines how teachers of as high a quality as possible were recruited or trained as teachers for SAPP. It is important to remember that in January 1973 there was only one trained agriculture teacher in the country, so we asked ourselves: 'wherever could we start?!!' This was indeed, a very great challenge!

Over the last century or more, there have been many observers who point to the quality of the teachers as a reason for the failure of an agricultural education programme in schools : inadequately trained teachers causing a descent either into drudgery or into a totally different objective of making money by selling produce. Sale of produce is of course an excellent outcome, but it must be a sideline from the essential educational objectives. Too often has the school garden become a source of vegetables for the teachers!!

The Kenya Institute of Education has suggested a more comprehensive range of qualities for an agriculture teacher than that listed above: personality; intelligence; physique; general education; wide interests; ability to plan; confidence; cooperativeness; courtesy; appearance and tidiness; rural background; training; continuation of professional development; good teacher-pupil relations; ability in self-evaluation. There was a suggestion that an ideal teacher needed to be both a teacher and a practical farmer. There was much debate throughout the period of the SAPP as to whether, in seeking staff for the programme, it was better to recruit trained agriculturalists and give them some teacher training, or trained teachers, and give them some agricultural instruction. The debate was somewhat theoretical since in practice it proved necessary to recruit from a wide range of backgrounds, not necessarily ideal!

During the SAPP, a number of aspects of policy regarding teachers became apparent: recruitment and selection; pre-service training; in-service training; staff development; the selection and training of counterpart teacher trainers (at the University); and assistance to teachers within the schools; and, not least, the level of pay in comparison with other teachers and with alternative employment opportunities.

> Research shows that there is only half as much variation in student achievement between schools as there is among classrooms in the same school. If you want your child to get the best education possible, it is more important to **get him assigned to a great teacher** than to a great school.
>
> **Bill Gates**

Recruitment and selection of teachers

Recruitment of teachers was clearly one of the essential pre-requisites before the programme could start. Two policy decisions were made by the Panel in 1972 - first, that every effort would be made to recruit expatriate teachers of

Agriculture from any possible source; and secondly, only qualified teachers would be employed. The interpretation of 'qualified' was left to the writer in his capacity as effective Senior Inspector for Agriculture, but in practice all teachers employed during the SAPP fell within one of the following categories: qualified teachers of agriculture with a degree or diploma in agriculture and teacher training; a diploma or a degree in agriculture; a degree in some related subject such as science or geography.[38]

Teaching load

The teaching load for academic subjects considered normally acceptable in Swaziland schools was thirty periods of forty minutes per week. The Panel recommended to headmasters that Agriculture teachers should have a maximum of 24 periods per week due to their much greater extra-mural responsibilities, such as supervision of poultry and rabbits and regular watering of the garden. In practice, it was not always possible for schools to adhere to this. For example, in a school with two streams, by the third year there would be a need for 30 periods to be taught. It was often difficult to provide a second teacher and so the existing teacher would have to exceed the recommended load.

Recruitment of existing non-Agriculture teachers

When it was apparent that seven schools would be starting the programme, two of the schools were selected because they had teachers able to teach Agriculture. Two other schools were able to provide a qualified teacher – one the only fully qualified Agriculture teacher, and the other who recruited an expatriate. For the other three schools, the International Voluntary Service (IVS) of the United Kingdom had promised to find three teachers, but were only able to find one in time for the first term. Another teacher from Johannesburg was recruited but only lasted for two weeks because her two children were unable to cope with learning in siSwati at the local primary school! Fortunately, a science teacher from the US Peace Corps agreed to teach

---

[38] There was only one exception to this: a teacher of history who had been brought up on a farm, had twenty years of teaching experience and was recommended by the school manager.

Agriculture. The remaining school was unable to start until the second term when a teacher from IVS arrived.

This was a difficult start, but in subsequent years, apart from occasional shortages, the recruitment situation improved. A large number of colleges and universities (18), volunteer organizations (15) and others (4) were approached in order to achieve the teacher supply required. Two local teachers with an Agriculture diploma were recruited in 1975, and one in 1976. A total of 48 teachers taught Agriculture during the period of the SAPP at the nineteen schools. Of these, seven were local citizens.

In 1977, after the completion of the pilot project, the first group of nine Swazi teachers qualified with a Diploma in Agricultural Education from the Faculty of Agriculture of the University of Swaziland (now Eswatini). In 1978, a further fourteen teachers qualified and in 1979 another twenty Swazis. Also fourteen US Peace Corps volunteers were recruited in January 1978, and the teacher supply situation therefore appeared assured. The Senior Inspector (who had been appointed in 1975) stated that he expected the teaching force to be 90% localized by 1981.

One important aspect of recruitment of local teachers, whether directly with diplomas in agriculture, or indirectly through the University into the Diploma in Agricultural Education, was the question of financial incentive. Teachers were on a lower scale than comparable recruits into the Ministry of Agriculture. This problem was overcome initially by allowing the agriculture teachers to enter the teaching service one grade up in comparison with other teachers on the grounds that they were technically qualified. The important issue here is related to status: However the problem is overcome, it is important to ensure that agriculture teachers are recognized as well qualified and that they should be suitably rewarded.

In-service training

The initial training course was held immediately before the first term started and lasted two weeks. The subjects covered were: resource materials, tools, logistics, teaching methods, teaching materials (practical), livestock in Swaziland, audio-visual aids, vegetable production, crop practical, farm mechanization, extension, and for the last three days, seminars and discussions led by two visiting specialists from UK who were very experienced in agriculture in schools in other African countries. The main topics were presented by a team of eleven from the University and Research Station. Subsequently, throughout the SAPP, a workshop lasting three days was held in January and September each year. Headmasters of all participating schools were invited to all these workshops since their understanding and cooperation was essential to the success of the programme. Although teachers were expected to attend, many of the expatriate teachers did not attend or only attended some sessions. Local teachers and headmasters, and particularly primary teachers, were more reliable. At the workshop in January 1976, an evaluation of

Localize.

At Independence from the United Kingdom in 1968, the majority of administrative and teaching posts throughout the country were occupied by expatriates. This situation continued for several years because, particularly in more senior positions, experience was necessary before local citizens were able to take over responsibility. In 2010, (37 years after the start of the SAPP) the World Bank financed a study of the Education System in Swaziland, of which the sub-title was *Training and Skills Development for Shared Growth and Competitiveness.* Much progress had been made by that date, but there was still a need for further development of the skills development sector.

the teaching materials was initiated which was a very important move forward since by this time there was a team of teachers who were experienced and able to make constructive contributions to the improvement of the programme.

Another aspect related to in-service training was the production periodically of a newsletter circulated to all Agriculture teachers by the Panel. This contained information concerning recommendations, prices and other technical data; suggestions for practical activities and construction of gadgets; and details of arrival and departure of teachers, and other social information

Pre-service training

Swaziland had a policy to localize (see box above) Government and private sector posts by the end of the 1990s, and so a training programme for teachers of Agriculture was regarded by the Panel as a very high priority. Even as early as 1970, the staff of the Faculties of Agriculture and Education gave thought to possible structures of such training. Three alternatives were considered: first, diplomates in Agriculture could be given a one year course in Agricultural Education; secondly, holders of a Secondary Teachers' Certificate could be given a one-year training in Agriculture; or thirdly a course in which Agriculture and Education courses would be given over the same period. The third option was considered most satisfactory for two reasons: first, it was sounder for students to learn about Agriculture at the same time as teaching skills. It was more satisfactory in terms of the options which would exist for structuring the course so that trainees could be adequately prepared for teaching practice. It would mean that students would be committed to a teaching career which was advantageous in terms of student motivation. Secondly, the Faculty of Agriculture was about to introduce a two year diploma in agriculture to replace the former three year diploma in agriculture. By adopting the third option, it would be possible to train Agriculture teachers in two years, rather than three years for either of the first two options. This would be cheaper, and would put the diploma on an equal standing with alternatives. A longer course in agricultural education than in agriculture or in teacher training at the teacher training college would be a disincentive to recruitment. Preliminary thoughts about the structure of the course proposed that time allocation should be in the proportion two thirds agriculture, one third education. The proposal to establish a Diploma in Agricultural Education was approved by the Council of the University in April 1973. In 1974, the Swedish International Development Agency (SIDA), through FAO[39], agreed to finance the diploma for an initial five years, after which the three Governments supporting the University agreed to finance the programme. Projections of student output for the period from 1977 to 1980 estimated 14 students per year. Actual output was much higher than this, from 16 rising to 32 students per year. This level of output was

---

[39] The Food and Agriculture Organization of the United Nations.

intended to supply teachers for Botswana and Lesotho as well as Swaziland. These proposals defined three objectives of the programme: first, to prepare teachers of agriculture for junior secondary schools; secondly, to do this in such a way that diplomates would be able to assist other rural development workers in the general task of raising the standard of living in the rural areas; and thirdly, to enable the diplomates to contribute to the teaching of other science based subjects in the schools.

During 1977 and 1978, an Agricultural Education Centre was developed at the Faculty of Agriculture, designed to contain all facilities which were likely to be found in schools. It also contained a Resource Centre in which equipment and visual aid materials were available for use by both students and qualified teachers on training courses. A Technician in Agricultural Education, whose main role was to assist with practical instruction, was appointed in 1976.

These developments are described here because they were an integral part of the development initiated during the SAPP. The first output of qualified teachers of Agriculture was in May 1977, so they were not able to contribute to the project in the first four years.

Training of Project Staff

There were two groups of staff for whom training was required. First, there was the staff of the project itself, and secondly the further education of counterpart teacher trainers. When the SAPP was about to be initiated in 1972, a diplomate in Agriculture of the Faculty of Agriculture, was recruited to the staff of the William Pitcher Teacher Training College[40]. His duties at the College were limited to teaching for one day a week. For the remainder of the time, he was concerned with the SAPP. During April and May 1973, a study tour was arranged for this team member to visit England, Kenya and Malawi under the auspices of the British Council, but owing to problems over funding he was unable to visit Malawi. The objective of this tour was to enable him to observe methods of teaching Agriculture in other countries which were more developed than Swaziland in this respect. In October 1974, he started the

---

[40] This was Mr. Themba Mazibuko. He possessed a Primary Higher Certificate and had been a teacher for 14 years, the last four years as a headmaster before entering the Diploma in Agriculture course in 1967. Because of this background, he was able to provide considerable assistance during the initial SAPP years.

Associateship in Teacher Education Overseas at the Institute of Education, University of London, studying at Garnett College Roehampton, South London, and completing it in September 1975. He then transferred to the University of Hull where he completed an M.A. degree in Education in September 1976. After his return he was technically a member of staff of William Pitcher Teacher Training College, but in fact was working very closely with the Senior Inspector for Agriculture.

In October 1978, one potential teacher trainer, who had completed the Diploma in Agricultural Education in 1977 with a credit, was sent to the University of the Philippines to, study for a B.Sc. in Agricultural Education financed by FAO.[41]. The Technician in Agricultural Education referred to above (Professor Comfort Mndebele, now retired) completed several degrees (Ph.D., M.Sc., M.A., and B.Sc.) at U.S. universities and became the Head of Department of Agricultural Education and Extension in succession to Professor Barnabas Dlamini.

These training activities have been described in some detail to emphasize the importance of developing staff at all levels as a very high priority in a project of this nature.

---

[41] This was Professor Barnabas Dlamini, who completed his doctorate at the University of West Virginia, and became head of the Department of Agricultural Education at the University of Swaziland. He was the pro Vice Chancellor at one point during his career, and sadly died at a young age.

CHAPTER TEN

Supervision and Support

The report of the World Conference on Agricultural Education and Training held in 1970 regarded '*the planning of agricultural education at national level*'as a priority. Other writers have commented on the necessity for a

> Education is the most powerful weapon you can use to change the world
> **Nelson Mandela**

centrally planned support organization for school agriculture, but most countries in Africa have done very little to implement these ideas. The administrative structure of the SAPP developed from having no full time staff at the beginning to having a Senior Inspector for Agriculture, four coordinators (inspectors), two curriculum writers (one each for primary and secondary), a

driver and a general assistant, at the end, a total of seven professional and two support staff. This chapter describes the building up of this team, the central facilities development, and the functions performed.

The Senior Inspector (Agriculture)

At the beginning, the writer fulfilled the role of Senior Inspector for Agriculture in the Ministry of Education[42]. Apart from assistance in preparing curriculum materials as outlined above, he received very substantial help from the Organizer

> **SCHOOL GARDEN SCHEME**
>
> This Nutrition project under the Ministry of Agriculture had been functioning since 1969, and had funds to purchase sets of tools for a limited number of schools each year. By agreement with the Organizer, they were in fact supplied to five of the initial group of schools.

---

[42] He was employed by the University of Swaziland but was fully supported by the University in carrying out these activities.

of the School Garden Scheme. The lecturer appointed to the Teacher Training College (Themba Mazibuko) referred to above, became the first coordinator. In 1974, a Poultry Officer[43] working for the Ministry of Agriculture became the second coordinator. At about the same time, two professional officers were appointed, technically to the staff of Swazi National High School, but in fact as Curriculum Writer (see box) and the third Coordinator (see box on next page). In March 1975, an officer was appointed by the British Ministry of Overseas Development (MOD) to function as curriculum writer and administrator of British Funds which were assisting in the development of the project. This designation was due to the fact that the MOD had been requested to supply staff some two years earlier and in the meanwhile, Mr. Watson had been appointed. What was needed at this point was a Senior Inspector and it was agreed that he should become Senior Inspector for Agriculture, responsible for the whole programme.[44]

The writer went on leave for two months in May 1975 shortly after the arrival of Mr. Teale, and so it was agreed that the responsibility for the SAPP would be transferred to Mr. Teale. In June 1975, the pressure of expansion became such that the Senior Inspector transferred to the Panel

---

Mr. J. Merryne. Watson, O.B.E., Curriculum Writer

Merryne Watson was a former member of staff at the Faculty of Agriculture who had retired. The Principal Secretary, Ministry of Education, Mr. Dlamini, had been taught Botany at the University in Lesotho by Mr. Watson, and enthusiastically agreed to this arrangement. Mr. Watson shared a house with the writer for about 18 months producing many of the modules. The writer was able to have direct access to the Principal Secretary because he was not strictly a member of staff of the Ministry!

---

[43] Mr. Duke Dube.

[44] Mr. Chris Teale was a very experienced teacher who had worked for some year in Zambia. The writer had asked Mr. Teale to apply for the post.

a teacher who had been teaching Agriculture at Ebenezer School[45]. He became the fourth coordinator.

In January 1975, the services of a general assistant were offered to the Panel by the Ministry of Education and this officer assisted in duplication of training materials, weighing out of materials and delivery of inputs. With the increasing burden of deliveries, it became apparent that a full time driver was required, and in August 1975, a driver was recruited.

Development of the central facilities

Central facilities[46] developed were in two categories: transport and buildings. First, transport. At the beginning of the SAPP, the School Gardens Scheme (SGS) had two vehicles and these were largely used for the SAPP by the Organizer (SGS) and the lecturer at the Teacher Training

Mr Giles Roques. Third coordinator. The writer had met Giles some months before in Zululand and told him what we were trying to do in teaching agriculture in schools. He was trying to develop a project in Zululand. I invited him to come and visit me in Swaziland if his plans did not work out. I was nevertheless rather surprised when he arrived at my house one evening with his wife, and plans to develop a farm nearby. I asked him to become a coordinator with the scheme if we could persuade the Principal Secretary (PS). The following morning, we went to the PS and Giles was appointed to the Swazi National High School, but worked full time on the SAPP. He became Senior Inspector and later joined the University to train the teachers. He was a man of great talent and enthusiasm who contributed enormously to the success of the SAPP. He died at a tragically young age. **DOMG**

---

[45] This was Mr. John Kay.

[46] 'Central' means facilities that were not specific for individual schools, but for the use of the whole programme.

College (effectively one of the coordinators). The writer's large Station Wagon made a contribution to carry heavy materials to schools.

In April 1974, one of these vehicles ceased to function! Funds had been raised (Schools Agriculture Panel Fund)47 for the purchase of a four wheel drive vehicle, but in the light of the secondment of the Poultry Officer (second coord-inator) there was a need for two vehicles. The funds for the four wheel drive veh-icle were very nearly enough to buy two two-wheel vehicles, but there was a shortfall of E1000. With the support of the Ministry of Education, an approach was made to the Ministry of Finance who made a special grant of E1000!

In July 1974, the Land Cruiser from the School Gardens Scheme reverted to that project. The appointment of a fourth

> **CURRICULUM DEVELOPMENT CENTRE**
>
> Initially, it was known as 'The Staff Room' because both Merryne and Giles were theoretically staff at Swazi National High School!

coordinator in June 1975 necessitated the purchase of another vehicle, and in September funds were raised for a Light Delivery Vehicle. Finally, in September 1976, a Land Cruiser and a five ton lorry were purchased, making a total at the end of the SAPP of four LDVs and one lorry. With the exception of the R1000 from the Ministry of Finance, all these purchases were made with funds raised by the Schools Agriculture Panel Fund.

Buildings

The building space for storage and development of curriculum materials was originally at the Faculty of Agriculture. The first set of curriculum materials was made using a borrowed duplicator in a classroom. When term started, this room was needed for a new class and the headquarters moved into a tobacco grading shed! This provided adequate storage space for curriculum materials, paper, furniture, garden and workshop tools, chemicals, fertilizers, seeds and some building materials – until the roof was blown off in a storm in November

---

47 Later, this became the Schools Agriculture Trust.

1976. The following morning the writer awoke to discover that his garage had been taken over as the Curriculum Development Centre for the SAPP until a new centre was developed at the Swazi National High School. Several large stores were used respectively for tools, fertilizers and chemicals, textbooks, handbooks and other curriculum materials, and one for sundry items. Some time later, a facility was developed adjacent to Emlalatini Development Centre in Ezulwini where materials, equipment, vehicles etc. could be stored and there was a facility for meetings[48].

> **DISCIPLINE**
> The formidable appearance (Mr. Teale was 6 feet 7 inches, 2 metres 66 cm tall) and directness of the Senior Inspector were usually sufficient to correct any irregularities, and only on two occasions was it necessary to take matters further. On one occasion, a builder who had constructed a workshop whose dimensions were grossly different from those in the plan was dismissed. On another occasion, financial irregularities were discerned, and the headmaster was posted to another school.

The functions of the central staff

These functions may be considered under two headings: supervisory and administrative. There were five supervisory functions.

Supervision of construction. This was the workshop/store; poultry house and rabbitry and the installation of irrigation facilities where required. This was necessary for three reasons: first, because these developments usually took place before an Agriculture teacher was appointed; secondly, because the materials were purchased centrally and any other plan would have been much more difficult to administer; and thirdly because coordinators possessed skills in these areas, which the school administrations and teachers generally did not. A builder was employed at each school and materials were delivered as required

---

[48] This is referred to in the telephone directory as the 'Schools Agriculture Panel office'!

by transport arranged by the coordinators. Headmasters, or agriculture teachers if appointed, were requested to supervise, but regular supervisory visits were made by the coordinators. This proved to be a very time-consuming activity but was regarded as essential if these developments were to be correctly carried out.

Distribution. This included tools, furniture and other equipment which had to be carried out at the beginning of each year. Thereafter, regular deliveries of textbooks, handbooks, lime, fertilizer, seeds, chemicals, livestock and feeds also had to be carried out or organized by the coordinators. After the first year, all these expendable materials had to be paid for and this necessitated invoicing and collection of funds. As the scheme expanded, so this function became of major importance in the time allocation of the coordinators, especially in January and February, and again in July and August. Feed deliveries were necessary in some schools throughout the academic year.

Advisory. This was probably the most important of all functions and yet pressure of the duties described above tended to make the coordinators' visits to schools very brief. During his period as temporary Senior Inspector, the writer found that teachers would pour out their problems and one or two hours per school to advise on problems was a real necessity. The coordinators were frequently criticized for not spending enough time carrying out this function. Throughout the SAPP teachers and coordinators have expressed the view that the proper function of the coordinators is advisory, and that to relieve them of the function of delivering goods, more drivers should be employed. They have often been described as the highest paid delivery boys (or girls) in the country! This was not due to any lack of desire on the part of the coordinators to provide help, but simply due to the extreme pressure of work with the first two duties discussed above.

Inspection. The Coordinators (who subsequently were called 'Inspectors') and the Senior Inspector had an inspection function. There were several occasions on which headmasters misappropriated materials intended for schools agriculture, such as the workshop being used as a classroom and fencing materials put around the school boundary; or teachers had borrowed tools for their own gardens. By inspection, or even by the threat of a stocktake, it was usually possible to put these problems right (see box above). But nevertheless, as with the advisory function, the extent to which the coordinators were able to fill this role was severely limited.

Organization of teachers' workshops and school visits. The coordinators were responsible for the general organization of these three day workshops normally held at William Pitcher Teacher Training College, including invitation of visiting speakers.

The coordinators met every two weeks at the Ministry of Education headquarters to discuss policy and to plan. They issued to all schools a list of the dates of planned visits to schools, between one and five schools being visited per day[49], with approximately three visits per school per term. In practice it was not always possible to adhere exactly to these schedules due to emergencies in other schools or breakdown of transport. School visit log books were kept so that a picture would be built up of the situation in each school. These log books were kept centrally.

Administrative responsibilities

Raising of Finance. The raising of finance and control of its expenditure was one of the most important functions of the central staff. Each year, the amount of capital and recurrent funds available was notified by the Chief Accountant of the Ministry of Education to the Senior Inspector who kept a Vote Book. In this, all orders with estimated costs were recorded. Later, invoices were submitted to the Senior Inspector (or his staff, the coordinators), recorded in the Vote Book and approved for payment by the Treasury through the Accounts Department of the Ministry of Education. This sounds simple, but proved to be very time consuming.

---

[49] Depending on physical distribution.

School selection. This process has been described above, and no problems were encountered. At the time of writing, some 45 years after the start of the SAPP, almost every secondary and high school is conducting a School Agriculture programme and this responsibility has fallen away. Only a small number of urban schools without adequate space have been unable to start a Modern Agriculture programme. See box above.

Publicity. It was regarded as very important to inform the public, the teaching profession, parents and any other groups concerned with agricultural and rural development about what was happening in the SAPP. In December 1972, a press conference was held at the

Number of schools teaching Agriculture in 2005
The Senior Inspector's Report in December 2005 showed the following figures for schools in which Agriculture was taught:
Primary schools: 286
Junior Secondary Schools 127
Senior Secondary Schools: 97
Pre-vocational Education: 16

Ministry of Education to which a wide range of persons was invited including a representative of His Majesty the King, representatives of Ministries, the University, the private sector, the press and broadcasting service, as well as the US Embassy and the British High Commission. An outline of the approach taken in introducing this subject in schools was described by a member of the Panel. Over the period of the SAPP, several articles were written for the Swaziland Teachers' Journal and several other regional and international journals. Over the next few years, samples of the textbooks were sent to 24 countries, largely in Africa. On several occasions, the Panel was asked to participate in the annual Swaziland Trade Fair.

Committee membership. The Senior Inspector was a member of several ministerial committees, most notably the curriculum coordinating committee and the regional panel for examinations. Membership of these panels was the formal channel of communication between the Senior Inspector for Agriculture and all the other subjects within the Ministry of Education. The hierarchy of responsibilities is described in Chapter 4 on Page 27.

<u>Overall development of the SAPP and beyond</u>. The Senior Inspector and his staff of coordinators and curriculum writers were responsible for formulating ideas; proposing and implementing structures of administration and other detailed aspects of the development of agricultural teaching in schools.

CHAPTER ELEVEN

Assessing Learning Outcomes –the Examination System

The educational system in Swaziland (as in most countries throughout the world) tends to be orientated towards achievement in examinations. Pupils are primarily concerned throughout their school lives with success in passing end of term or end of year examinations. Because success is measured by pupils and parents in these terms, teachers tend to be similarly influenced. The quality of the

SWAZILAND EXAMINATIONS COUNCIL

Until 1975, the Schools Examinations Council (for Botswana, Lesotho and Swaziland) (SEC) was based in Lesotho. Over the next few years, this arrangement broke up and current responsibility for this level of examination is held by the Swaziland Examinations Council.

actual learning experience very often takes second place to good performance in the examinations. While these two aspects of education should be by no means incompatible, excessive concern for the second may result in insufficient care about the first. The design of the examination system is therefore of great importance in influencing teachers to pay sufficient attention to the quality of the learning experiences of the pupils. The following section describes the structure of the examination system in Swaziland, notably at the Junior Certificate level (three years of secondary education), and outlines the design of examinations at that level in Agriculture, a design which was adopted in an attempt to encourage teachers to use methods of teaching which would enable the objectives of teaching the subject to be achieved. It then analyses the actual achievements in the first four years in which the examination was taken. During the period of the SAPP, public examinations were taken at three levels in the Swaziland school education system, and each was conducted by a different authority. The first, conducted by the Ministry of Education, was at the end of Standard Five, after seven years of primary education. The second was the Junior Certificate, after three years of secondary education, conducted by the

Schools Examinations Council of the University of Botswana, Lesotho and Swaziland (see box above). The third level (Form Five) was the Cambridge Overseas School Certificate, after a further two years of secondary education, and was conducted by the Local Examinations Syndicate of the University of Cambridge, UK.

Already in existence at the Form Five level was a syllabus called 'Agricultural Science' offered by Cambridge and two high schools presented candidates for this examination. The Panel considered that this syllabus was too science orientated and insufficiently practical to fill the current needs and did not follow on from the material covered in the Junior Certificate syllabus.

This book is concerned primarily with the Junior Certificate syllabus and the examination which was conducted by the Schools Examinations Council. An Examiner and Moderator were appointed by the Council. The Examiner's duty was to set an examination paper and a memorandum of marking and, assisted by markers appointed by him or her, to mark the scripts. The duty of the Moderator was to check the paper set by the Examiner as regards level of difficulty, whether it covered the syllabus and whether the memorandum of marking was correct, and to check the marking of selected scripts. Different examinations were developed for each of the three countries, and this would replace the old syllabus. The School certificate Level syllabus was not developed until several years later.

The great difficulty which was faced at this point was how to get away from only a written examination, and to give credit for acquisition of practical skills. The structure which emerged was as follows:

> Standardized testing is at cross purposes with many of the most important purposes of public education. It doesn't measure big picture learning, critical thinking, perseverance, problem solving, creativity or curiosity, yet those are the qualities great teaching brings out in a student.
>
> **Randi Weingarten**

Junior Certificate Examination (three hours, 50%)

- 100 multiple choice questions: 25% of marks. Pass mark 34%

- Short answer questions: 100 marks. 25% of marks Pass mark34%.

Running Assessment (50%)

- Practical assessment: 25%; Teacher, moderated once by Examiner.
- Tests, projects, assignments, workbooks etc. 25%: teacher and moderated once by Examiner.

Teachers were provided with a paper which described in detail how marks were to be allocated for the practical assessment: Fifty marks for crop-related skills (see box below) and 50 marks for livestock skills; for livestock, ten marks each for handling skills, husbandry skills, results, record keeping and enthusiasm/attitude. Each of these headings was described in detail. (See example in box) Land Preparation and Planting covered marking out, fencing, digging, preparing seedbeds, sowing direct, transplanting, spacing, row distances. Enthusiasm/attitude covered: punctuality, hard work, reliability, cooperation with the teacher and fellow pupils, extra-curricular work. A score out of ten was described as follows:

> **MARKS FOR CROP RELATED SKILLS**
> Land preparation and planting (10)
> Maintenance (10)
> Results (10)
> Record keeping (10)
> Enthusiasm/attitude (10)

1: **Very poor.** Rarely given; 2-4: **Poor.** Fail; 5: **Marginal**; 6: **Satisfactory**; 7-9: **Above average**; 10: **Outstanding.** Rarely given.

Essay type questions were excluded from the examination structure because answering this type of question depends very much on linguistic ability and this is not a skill with which we are primarily concerned in an Agricultural Education course. Pupils are often limited by their inability to express themselves in writing and this should be avoided in an Agriculture examination.

Although these detailed guidelines on the preparation of continuous assessment grades were distributed to teachers in 1975, in practice, due to rapid turnover of teachers, insufficient care in maintaining records in schools, changes of headmasters and other reasons - probably insufficient training of teachers - this sort of information was rarely available when the examiner went round the schools. How to ensure a genuine grading of practical ability continues to be a challenge. In 1977 moderation of continuous assessment was carried out by the Coordinators in addition to the Examiner. In each school where records were inadequate, one technique used was to interview five poor, five medium and five good candidates, based on the lists submitted by the teachers, and to ask questions related to practical skills. This whole system of examination was very time consuming and with increased numbers of schools and candidates, some methods of simplifying were sought. A test was carried out in one school and it was found that the performance of pupils in answering multiple choice and short answer questions were highly significantly correlated. Therefore, one simplification is to use only multiple choice questions which are easier to mark. Unfortunately, this does not mitigate the difficulty of having a fair and effective system of assessing practical skills.

In 1975, the first year when the examination was conducted in the initial schools, the results were astonishing with the following distribution:

A 189; B 81; C 22; D 0; F 1

In the subsequent two years, results were more spread, but there were still very few pupils earning less than a D grade. These results are so good that there is very little incentive for the teachers to try very hard or for the pupils to work.

A number of conclusions must be drawn from these initial results. Doubt must be cast on the accuracy of the published results. The possibility of upwardly inflating the results exists. One might ask whether this matters, but it must be emphasized that it is of the utmost importance to the success of the whole programme that the examination results should accurately reflect the achievements of the pupils. This is so because it is important that pupils should not consider themselves to be better than they are. With this sort of result, Agriculture would be seen as a soft option. One of the most important reasons for concern is that such an outcome may destroy the morale and enthusiasm of even the most dedicated teacher. If a good teacher sees that his idle colleague in another school is able to achieve equally good results, he may well be tempted to give up making the extra effort which is certainly needed to make the mediocre school programme into a good one, and the good one into an outstanding one.

CHAPTER TWELVE

Evaluating the Outcomes from SAPP

Introduction

By definition, evaluation is designed to measure the value added by an activity or programme. Evaluation may be summative – drawing conclusions when an activity has been completed, or it may be formative – identifying ongoing problems or challenges that may be corrected and then fed into a programme as it continues and develops. Both types of evaluation were used as SAPP progressed and a number of agencies were engaged in the evaluation process. From the outset, it was agreed that all aspects should be tracked with a view to refining its content and activities. Regular meetings of the core staff involved in the programme reviewed issues and challenges as they arose, a kind of formative evaluation. But it was also felt that a more rigorous and formal approach to evaluation should be adopted, using external and impartial expertise. A total of five evaluations were therefore carried out by different agencies over the life-time of SAPP.

An initial evaluation of schools was carried out in which it was found that teachers were mainly under the age of 36, largely from the USA and Britain, well qualified, but limited in experience. Age of the pupils ranged from 12 years to 21[50] and class sizes from 32 to 49. Important constraints included provision of adequate water, fencing of gardens and the provision of appropriate tools. Also examined were arrangements for disposal of produce, and storage facilities at schools. All school committees, teachers of other subjects and Chiefs had responded enthusiastically to the introduction of Modern Agriculture. The rural junior secondary schools, were small with, for the most part, inexperienced and constantly changing staff. They were distant from supplies and markets and were newly established and therefore ill-equipped and lacking in well-established procedures for administration. It was surprising that SAPP was accepted with such enthusiasm. The lack of facilities was as expected and the more difficult problems – land and irrigation - were minimized by selecting schools with minimum problems.

---

[50] Over-age pupils were a common feature owing to lack of funds by families.

Achievement of objectives. The SAPP was started in a geographically widespread though limited number of schools (initially seven), rapidly spreading throughout the country[51]. The first step was to develop learning objectives: knowledge and understanding; attitudes and mental skills, and practical skills:

Knowledge and understanding of: Human nutrition; animal nutrition, breeding, housing, disease control and handling; Crop nutrition, varieties, cultivation, pest control harvesting and storage; pasture management; conditions affecting plant and animal growth; issues related to forestry and fisheries; agro-ecological zones, land tenure, development projects; career opportunities in farming and associated technologies.

Attitudes toward: modern farming and its relationship to scientific research; awareness of economic principles in relation to profitability; awareness of environmental, pollution and conservation issues; appreciation of rural development workers' activities.

Mental or Cognitive skills: interpretation of farm records; ability to assemble information and make management decisions; ability to carry out basic farm calculations; ability to apply knowledge to practical situations.

Practical skills: Skills in vegetable and crop production; Skills in poultry, rabbit and other livestock production; Use and care of agricultural implements; Skills in keeping farm records.

Against this list of desirable knowledge, attitudes and skills, nineteen modules were prepared. As the modules were developed, so the objectives of each module were developed and were included in the Teachers' Handbook. It was important to determine whether these objectives were being achieved. Since many of the objectives were difficult to assess, a number of approaches were used.

Approaches to evaluation of achievement of objectives

A baseline survey of students was carried out to determine the initial level of knowledge, skills and attitudes of pupils in the SAPP schools compared with

---

[51] By 1978 there were 31 schools offering Modern Agriculture. There were 217 junior and senior secondary (high) schools at that time. . At the time of writing (2018), nearly every secondary and high school was offering 'Modern Agriculture', with the exception of some urban schools with no land.

those in three other rural school. Three years later, a similar test was administered, as far as possible with the same school population. The result indicated that the Modern Agriculture pupils had improved significantly more.

Comparison. The second approach was to make a comparison between the old Agricultural Science curriculum and Modern Agriculture. The pass rate in Modern Agriculture had improved greatly over the passes in the old syllabus. In round terms, total passes in Agricultural Science between 1969 and 1973 were between 57 and 74 per cent. This compares with Modern Agriculture between 1975 and 1977 with 100% pass rates. This comparison can be heavily criticized, but it does support the hypothesis stated above.

IVS survey. The third evaluation was carried out by the International Voluntary Service (IVS) who had supplied many of the teachers. A questionnaire was circulated to all Agriculture teachers, of whom 55% thought that the course 'taught practical farming'. Some interesting comments were made including: '*The pupils can't put much into practice because they have not got the capital to start commercial farming.' 'There should be more emphasis on improving subsistence farming.' 'The scale is too small.' 'Much of the practical farming is derived from European agriculture.' Students have very little awareness of business in agriculture, nor are they interested in continuing in what they see as a 'demeaning career*'. 75% thought that the course 'demonstrated business aspects of farming' and 80% that it provided general knowledge, but there was a lack of information about career opportunities in agriculture. The overall rather subjective conclusion drawn from these responses indicated that the teachers felt that considerable knowledge was acquired, but there was a long way to go!

Evaluation from the teachers' viewpoint. The fourth evaluation was a test conducted with 53 Modern Agriculture teachers in 1978 (five years after the programme had started). This test was kept short to encourage a good response. The questions were in five groups of teachers' opinions: the extent to which objectives had been achieved; Materials; Diploma training (for Swazi teachers only); In-service courses; and Examinations.

Responses were requested to the question: *To what extent has the course enabled pupils to acquire knowledge in the following areas*'. The areas corresponded to the module titles with some modules being joined together (farm records and business, and the two conservation modules). Overall, 8 of the modules were viewed very favourably at the 69% to 84% level, the remainder scored between 29% and 55% favourable opinion, while Machinery, Forestry and Plant science were judged the least successful in imparting knowledge. Within these figures there were significant differences in the perceptions of Swazi and non-Swazi teachers, especially regarding the Storage and Harvesting unit. The reason for the divergence of views between Swazi and non-Swazi (mostly American or British) teachers is almost certainly due to the difference in background, the non-Swazis looking at the situation in comparison with their own countries. These results certainly throw light on the quality of achievement with these initial modules. The more practical modules (vegetable and crop production and poultry) were much more successful with favourable ratings of 84%, 88% and 74%.

External evaluation. The fifth evaluation was carried out by a specialist team which visited Swaziland from the UK, which country was, by 1978, providing much of the funds for the SAPP[52]. Their terms of reference were to 'study all available evidence on the improvement of the teaching and learning of agriculture.' The Ministry of Education added to this some further terms of reference: that they should 'assess the success thus far of the project in terms of the objectives it set out to achieve.' Their reaction was generally favourable, but they were critical of certain aspects: *'the widely adopted teaching method to guide pupils reading in turn through chapter and verse of the unit which results in dull mechanical lessons ...the strict division made by most teachers between classroom and practical activities'*. There was a need for much greater emphasis on developing curriculum content and improving teaching methods. They proposed that the modules should be adjusted to include some compulsory and some optional units: Vegetable, crops, poultry, animal production and soil conservation would be compulsory; supported by farm records, animal nutrition, cattle in Swaziland and crop harvesting and storage. The remaining modules would be optional. It appears to be significant that the basic and supportive modules are the ones better received by the teachers.

---

[52] This team of two specialists was provided by TETOC, the Technical Education and Training Organization for Overseas Countries of the British Ministry of Overseas Development.

Some specific findings from the evaluations

Knowledge objectives. In the light of the findings from these evaluations it was agreed that a reduction in the amount of material to be covered would enable better levels of knowledge to be achieved. This could be achieved by introducing the idea of options and by deleting some modules of a lower priority. Some teachers were very enthusiastic about the practical aspects of the programme, but it is important that it should not become too narrow. Secondly, efforts were needed to improve the quality of teaching. There was clearly a need for much more in-service training. Much could also be achieved by strengthening the role of coordinators (inspectors) as advisers on methodology during regular visits. The role of the teachers' handbooks' in proposing methods of teaching should also be strengthened. Finally, the module text books should continue to be made more accurate, attractive and relevant. This is an on-going strategy.

Achievement of skill objectives. The skill objectives were in two groups: First, mental or cognitive skills including the keeping of farm records, calculations and decision making; and secondly, practical farm skills, relating chiefly to the more practical modules (although it was intended that practical activities should be used wherever possible.) The achievement of skills in these areas proved more difficult to evaluate. Many skills can only be tested over a period of time. This was the reason for allocating 25% of the marks to be given by the teachers as a running assessment. There were three forms of evaluation carried out:

Survey of teachers' views. Teachers were asked for their views, which produced comments such as: *'the scale is too small for realistic practical farming'*; In a pupil questionnaire a large proportion of pupils said that they found the practical work *'boring'*; a great majority felt that *'learning agriculture at school helped them with farming at home'*; many felt that not enough practical farming is taught; *shortage of time devoted to practical activities;* the teachers main complaint was with the practical side of the programme; school farms should be established to teach practical agriculture on a *larger and more realistic scale.* These comments, though not quantified, give an indication of teachers' views about the practical side of the course and, by implication, the level of skill acquisition. There were three main areas of criticism: (a) Because the course leads to examinations, teachers tend to concentrate on those activities most likely to lead to good examination results, which are generally not the practical ones; (b) The teachers consider that insufficient time is available to teach practical skills properly; and (c) In some cases lack of land and equipment was identified as a major concern.

These criticisms were felt to be unrealistic: there is little alternative to some sort of examination system; there is already a 25% allocation of marks for continuous assessment; time allocation recommended in the text books is already substantial; much of the theoretical aspects can be taught in a practical way; expanding practical activities is unrealistic and would create numerous logistical problems. However, it must be recognized that most of the teachers were inexperienced and would later on find ways of making things run more smoothly.

The first criticism regarding the examinations led to the conclusion that more emphasis needs to be given to training the teachers in conducting practical evaluation. Lack of time was clearly a problem and this can be tackled by cutting out some of the less essential modules. Lack of facilities and equipment is a problem which needs time to overcome. At the initial stages of the SAPP, funds were almost non-existent, but as time went on, it became possible to supply more adequate tools.

Secondly, a questionnaire was distributed to teachers asking the following question: *Has the course enabled pupils to acquire skills in the following areas?* The views were widely divergent between Swazis and non-Swazis. Nine categories of practical activity were considered: In vegetable production 81% of all teachers thought that much or very much had been achieved. This was one of the most successful modules. With record keeping, 69% of Swazis but only 7% of non-Swazis responded positively. With signs of erosion, 70% were favourable with a very wide divergence between Swazis (94%) and non-Swazis (43%). For the remainder, poultry keeping, rabbit keeping, reducing erosion and care of tools received at least 50% positive responses. Tree growing and budgeting were much less positive. There was a clear need on the part of teachers for improvements in the skills area. One suggestion was that in-service courses should be more skills orientated and school timetables should be arranged to give longer practical periods. Teachers were also much concerned about the inadequacies in the system of skills evaluation.

Thirdly, The TETOC evaluation did not refer specifically to skill acquisition, but they did come up with some helpful suggestions regarding an open-sided *'covered area'* for use by teachers to carry out demonstrations and briefings, and also in case of rain during classes. The poultry houses were thought to be too big resulting in too much time being spent on routine operations. The TETOC team did not like the use of rabbits as part of the programme because they were not being used properly for teaching purposes. It was originally intended that several alternatives could be used as examples for looking after livestock, such as pigs, sheep and goats, but rabbits are smaller, less expensive and generally easier to manage. It is true that rabbit meat is not well known to Swazis, but the main criticism is lack of markets, as well as difficulties in caring for rabbits during the vacations. The TETOC team wanted to see the vegetable and crop production units continued throughout all three years of the programme. However, this would result in a substantial curtailment of time available for other important modules. A further suggestion was the introduction of an account book for each school with information about expenses and income, first, to ensure that detailed information is available for inspection when necessary, and also because this can be used as a very valuable teaching aid in relation to the economic aspects of production. Finally, the TETOC team emphasized the need to use the practical activities to learn scientific facts and principles at least as much as routine feeding and watering. With increasing confidence, it is hoped that the teachers will take advantage of this opportunity.

<u>What did the evaluations tell us</u>? The evaluation of attitude change is a difficult task. A true estimate of changes in attitude needs a very clear idea about the initial attitudes in order to determine whether there really has been any measurable change. Any changes that are detected may have been brought about by a whole host of influences other than the SAPP. Attitude was defined as a positive or negative action tendency towards a person, a concept or an organization. Would people's actions regarding agriculture differ as a result of going through the SAPP? Several sources were used to determine any shift in attitudes. First, a survey was conducted in three schools. Respondents could answer on a four point scale, two favourable and two unfavourable. This questionnaire was pre-tested and then administered in February and again in

November 1976, and a third time in October 1978 in three schools. The results were as follows:

- Science. There was some improvement after one year but no significant change after that. This may be due to the fact that the latter part of the course had rather less emphasis on science;

- Conservation. With all the inadequacies of this test, it was encouraging to observe that although there was no improvement after one year (when the subject had not been studied) after the whole three years, there was a highly significant improvement when the subject had been studied in two modules.

- Rural development agencies. The responses were very varied, but the overall improvement in attitude was highly significant.

- Enjoyable. The initial attitude was fairly high, which is surprising if it is true that agriculture is generally held in low esteem. By the end of three years, there was generally a significant improvement as the pupils realized that agriculture involved more than cattle herding, bird watching, hoeing and other not very inspiring tasks.

- Worthwhile. The question was phrased to enquire about the importance of farming to the individual and to the nation. Responses varied substantially according to school. Boys reacted significantly more positively than girls, but the overall response was positive.

- Business. There was a significant improvement in most schools, but in one urban boys' school there was a highly significant and negative response. Probably these boys were looking towards urban employment.

- Total. This was looking at an overall attitude to farming and after three years the change was very significantly positive.

This questionnaire was designed to test changes of attitude to six aspects of farming in three schools, and after one and three years. Of importance is the fact that there was no significant change of attitude to business and science, which is a disappointing result.

A second test was carried out in five randomly selected schools testing attitudes to English, Science, Agriculture and Mathematics. The other three subjects were included principally as a diversion. There were six questions; the subject was:

- Easy/difficult

- Useless at home/ useful at home
- Important to Swaziland/unimportant to Swaziland
- Interesting/dull
- Useful for studying other subjects/ useless for this
- Helpful at work/not helpful at work

At the beginning, English received the highest response followed by Agriculture. The test was administered again after one and after three years. After one year, there was very little change, but after three years all schools showed a positive change towards agriculture as a subject, in three of the schools it was very highly significant.

A third evaluation was carried out with 24 of the teachers. They were asked what they considered had been achieved in relation to each module. 80% thought that the pupils enjoyed the course and were enthusiastic. 60% thought that the pupils came to see agriculture as worthwhile. 55% thought that the course stimulated positive attitudes to rural development and conservation. 85% thought that the overall objectives were good and 65% thought that the outcomes were realized. On the other hand, self-reliance, resourcefulness and problem solving ability were not taught effectively. The main criticism was too much book work, too much emphasis on examinations and on commercial agriculture, There was a need for careful thinking about how to rectify these valid criticisms. From these responses, we can draw a number of conclusions. First, there was a more positive response in relation to the knowledge, skill and attitude questions from Swazi teachers than from the expatriates. Secondly, the responses to questions about attitude appear to be realistic since only two questions received a positive response. Thirdly, the teachers were not very positive about the achievement of the intended outcomes. It is important to recognize that many of these outcomes (such as self-reliance, management skills, resourcefulness) are very difficult to judge and highly subjective.

Summary

This section has been concerned with the extent to which attitude changes have been achieved. Because of the difficulty associated with the evaluation of attitude change, a range of opinions was sought, both from pupils and teachers. It is difficult to summarize the achievements briefly as there are so many individuals and so many aspects of attitude. It is probably true to say that pupils feel more positive about agriculture and that SAPP has helped to bring about this improved attitude. Certain aspects of the programme (eg vegetable production) have received more positive responses but it is natural that some aspects of the subject will be more interesting and attractive to the learners. The overall impression gained from the series of evaluations of SAPP is one of limited achievement of a positive nature. It would appear that the provision of a programmed course with textbooks and handbooks, supply of materials required to carry out an effective teaching programme, the training of teachers, and employment of supervisors (coordinators or inspectors) has enabled many of the detailed objectives to be achieved. These other items in the SAPP are considered in the next chapter.

Regrettably, the effort to obtain views from former students was unsuccessful, despite advertisements placed in the 'Times of Swaziland' on two occasions, and efforts made through current agriculture teachers. The only response received came from a person who had become a part time farmer, but also a teacher of agricultural economics. He had found the course very useful in several jobs especially as a project officer, a director of statistics and a teacher. Clearly, the Modern Agriculture course had been a factor in his career development.

CHAPTER THIRTEEN

Beyond the classroom: Evaluation of the Support Services of SAPP

Although what happens in the classroom, the vegetable garden and the poultry house are key dimensions, a critical issue is that of support services and their effectiveness. The employment of a team tasked with professional and logistical support for the teaching and learning process was an essential element in the programme. This chapter outlines the evaluation of the services available to the teachers including supervision and support, the teaching materials, the tools, equipment and expendable materials.

Supervision and support

From the earliest days it was agreed that the production of teaching and learning materials, the provision of some tools, fencing, water for irrigation and other equipment would be a necessary but insufficient input to a major curricular change. In other school subject areas it might be enough to produce a new text-book, provide some in-service teacher preparation and then let any change take root. It should be noted that at this time in the history of Swaziland's educational development new approaches to mathematics teaching were being pioneered in selected schools, supported by a large expatriate team of mathematics experts. Similarly, the new subject of Development Studies was being developed and piloted by a UNDP team of foreign experts, to say nothing of the US funded redrafting of the primary school curriculum. Change and innovation were the norm but with an essentially practical subject like Modern Agriculture it was critical to provide a combination of supervision and advisory support in the field through a team of coordinators. Looking back at the earliest experiences a mental picture arises of a battered Government vehicle loaded down with fence poles, fertilizer bags and live chicks trundling along Swaziland's dusty roads attempting to reach a far-flung school before the end of the school day! Interaction with the teachers and their pupils led to the building up of a unique set of relationships between the coordinator team and the school communities they supported. The role of the coordinators (now called inspectors) is outlined in the chapter above, but it is important to recognize and emphasize that at this initial stage in the development of the

Modern Agriculture programme, and also on-going, this element of support to the teachers was absolutely – and continues to be – essential.

Although the team of 'hands on' coordinators managed the day-to-day logistics of support, it soon became apparent that a more substantial support structure would be necessary, in particular with a stronger emphasis on the advisory role. The TETOC evaluation made the very important proposal that the position of Senior Inspector should be established, as this would give confidence that the Government was fully committed to the Modern Agriculture programme. Further, they strongly recommended that the function of the Inspectors should clearly swing towards technical and professional support. This view was fully supported by the teachers who felt the need for much greater advisory support. This would enable the coordinators to carry out the most important tasks. There was an urgent need to expand the supervisory and administrative structure. The facilities for storage and distribution of inputs was improved by the development of a School Agriculture Centre which was well established in 1979.

Teaching materials

This includes the textbooks, teachers' handbooks, and other written materials and teaching aids. It was important to determine whether these materials contributed to the achievement of the objectives and to determine how they could be improved. This is a continuous process, and the text books have developed a long way from the original photocopied booklets.

Textbooks. A teachers' workshop was held in 1976 at which teachers were challenged to comment on various aspects of the project development. They agreed that the aims and objectives were sound, with just minor adjustments. They accepted the 'modular' approach to materials development. However, it was agreed that the amount of material to be covered was too extensive, thus the number of modules was reduced and a structure of basic and optional modules was adopted. These discussions resulted in a reduction in the number of modules, a change in the order of presentation and at a later stage, the TETOC report proposed that five modules should be 'basic', with four support units and six optional modules. Time allocation to the basic modules was increased. Agricultural education students were asked to rank the importance of modules and placed Vegetable and Crop Production first and second, followed by Conservation. Poultry and cattle came next, with animal health and machinery scoring high. A survey of teachers' opinion of the textbooks scored a 94% positive assessment.

Students of Agricultural Education at the University were asked to write essays on curriculum development and made several helpful suggestions as follows:

- Inserts should be prepared for the textbooks containing up-to-date information;
- The subject of simple farm technology should be introduced into the curriculum;
- Other topics suggested for inclusion were dairy, sheep, fruit, and agricultural economics;
- Less conventional topics were hygiene and handwork;
- Textbooks should be bound together in one volume for each year.

Some of the books were being used in Lesotho and the users considered that the books were easy to read, and the vocabularies were very useful. There were of course also some criticisms: the illustrations in the early editions were unclear; pagination was muddled; practical activities were inadequately described; the question and answer format of the text was used too much. One teacher thought that the curriculum attempted too much and suggested: *What a true contribution we could make if our students could leave us convinced of the need to conserve the soil, able to grow well those vegetables that contribute most to nutrition, able to produce a first class crop of maize, and sure of the practices which will keep the family herd disease and pest free and relatively well fed during the lean months.* This sentiment followed closely the recommendation of the TETOC report. The same teacher criticized the conservation module which contained no mention of storm water drains or gulley control. It may be that the teachers were either not well informed about some technical aspects or were disinclined to criticize.

Teachers' handbooks. These were originally intended to be part of the system and to be used alongside the textbooks. One of the most important aspects of the handbooks was that they suggested practical activities to illustrate points in the textbooks. A survey in 1979 showed that five teachers had not seen handbooks at all, and although 63% managed to find them 'adequate' there were no 'very good' respondents.

It is likely that the lack of emphasis on the teachers' handbooks resulted in a criticism from the TETOC evaluation: *Less impressive (than the principles) is the strict division made by most teachers between classroom and practical activities and the general absence of real expertise in the basic classroom crafts of questioning, enlightened use of the blackboard and the use of organic and other aids. We saw little attempt being made to teach in a lively applied manner. The widely adopted teaching method is for the teacher, book in hand, to guide pupils reading in turn through chapter and verse of the module textbook, which results in dull, mechanical lessons and passive, often bored pupils.* The TETOC team proposed the following remedial actions:

- The role of the coordinators/inspectors should be orientated much more strongly towards giving advice and pedagogical support – that is, 'teaching the teachers how to teach!'
- There should be a course on teaching methods first for the coordinators, and then for the teachers;
- The textbooks should be used only occasionally in class and teachers should present lessons in less formal and more practical manner

These were excellent suggestions, but the teachers' handbooks were originally designed to assist the teacher in achieving quality lessons, with method and content for each lesson clearly described. At the time, there was a clear need to revive or improve the use of the teachers' handbooks.

Other teaching aids. There were originally two other items: workbooks and work cards. They were both discontinued because of the cost and time needed to prepare them. The questions were, where appropriate, included in the textbooks.

Buildings and furniture

The buildings erected at schools had to serve several functions: laboratory, workshop, classroom, store, livestock housing. Their evolution is described above. Security was the most important factor which necessitated development of a solid building able to resist theft. The final arrangement was that there would be two buildings: a laboratory/ workshop, store, classroom and the other building which was a livestock house with room for poultry and rabbits with storage space for feeds. The TETOC team criticized the cost of the building, although when compared with the cost of classrooms or science laboratories, the price was actually very reasonable. The cost of setting up an agriculture unit including buildings, garden and workshop tools, furniture, irrigation, fencing, livestock and visual aids was E16 528. An ordinary classroom was E8590 and a science laboratory was E33660. Compared with these figures, the cost of setting up an Agriculture unit is comparatively low.

The suggestion was made of providing an open-sided covered area suitable for practical demonstrations, but such a building would be inadequate when a classroom space was needed. What is basically required is an adequate centre where the teacher can carry out instruction, practical activities and simple experimental work; where he can display graphic material as well as samples, growing plants and similar objects. Critical is the 'image' of agriculture as compared with other subjects such as science, and assurance of security.

Tools equipment and fencing

Some of the tools supplied in 1973 were of poor quality, notably hoes, rakes and forks. Subsequent purchases took account of the necessity for strong tools. Some schools looked after their tools better than others. The evaluation of irrigation equipment showed an exactly 50% split between those who thought it was satisfactory and those who thought otherwise. It was clear that teachers with initiative were often able to overcome problems with water provision in the garden. The TETOC team suggested that in some circumstances, the use of trickle irrigation would be worth attempting. Much of the fencing in the original schools was erected by the teacher and quality was variable. The TETOC team emphasized the need for expenditure in this vital facility.

Teachers

The qualities sought in the teaching and supervisory staff have been described. Most of these attributes are very complex and to evaluate them would be a difficult task. Also, the expatriate teachers were selected by the various bodies who sent them to Swaziland such as the US Peace Corps and British IVS. The few Swazis who were recruited in the early years for the most part had a Diploma in Agriculture but little or no teacher training. By the time of the 1979 evaluation, the target of replacing expatriate teachers with Swazis was nowhere near fulfilled. As there were many other jobs available for anyone with a diploma in agriculture and initially very few with a diploma in agricultural education, there was still at that date a shortage of teachers. It was stated that a need to recruit expatriate teachers would continue for some years. At the time of writing of this chapter (2018) the situation is entirely different. It would seem to be clear that a considerable in-service training programme was necessary owing to the inadequate training of many of the teachers during the initial stages. Now, most of the teachers have been trained at the Uneswa Faculty of Agriculture. The teacher response to the question 'are there sufficient in-service courses and workshop?' was a 67% no! Most teachers thought they were not long enough. Too much time was spent discussing problems in the schools. An open question inviting suggestions received a response that: Courses should be at least two weeks (they were actually 3 days); more practical; in a better location with practical facilities (that was the original intention of the construction at the Faculty of Agriculture of an 'Agricultural Education Centre'); more specialist talks were required; the inspectors should spend more time on preparation.

By 1979, three groups of trainees had completed the Diploma in Agricultural Education, but the three original lecturers had departed. There was a need to increase continuity in the teaching force at the university. Change has now (2018) slowed down greatly and this has given a much greater level of continuity. It is certainly correct that changes should take place to improve the quality of the training, and in 1978, a major revision of syllabi took place, starting with the Diploma in Agriculture. The effect on the Diploma in Agricultural Education was an increase in the husbandries, economics and land use, and an increase in training in teaching methods. Several new courses were introduced including nutrition, construction skills, communications and small livestock.

A survey of former students at the university, who were now teachers, showed that 80% considered that the course was too short (two years). 73% thought that the practical content was too little. However, 64% felt 'adequately prepared to start teaching.' The training of the staff of the Faculty of Agriculture who would be responsible for the diploma, and later, degree, in Agricultural Education, depended on availability of staff to send away for training, and of opportunities in various universities. In particular, the University of West Virginia played a very important role in making training available to several members of the current staff.

Examinations

The TETOC evaluation drew attention to the rather disconcerting fact that they had visited schools with run down or defunct livestock and garden units who had nevertheless managed to achieve good results in the examinations. In some cases, schools whose practical facilities were in disrepair were able to achieve much better results in the examinations. It would appear that some adjustments upward had been made when 100% pass was achieved, despite the Examiner's recommendation that 20% should fail. This sort of outcome would be very discouraging to conscientious teachers. There should therefore be much more careful moderation. Course marks should be moderated on a more continuous basis and not in a one-off at the end of the year. There was a need to develop a more appropriate system of examinations. Evaluation was carried out with the teachers and it may be concluded that there was a need for development of a more effective and accurate system of practical achievement evaluation. There should be a larger role for the moderator in interviewing pupils. It was clear that there would be a need for teachers to be trained in implementation of better practical examination techniques.

Summary

As with any curricular innovation, the gaps between the official curriculum, the curriculum as delivered in the classroom or workshop and the hidden curriculum absorbed by the pupils emerge as a result of reported experience and formal evaluation. What may seem a rational and logical approach to the teaching of agriculture, developed along professional and technically sound lines may, in practice, reveal fault-lines which were never anticipated. Few of these emerged and the basic structure of SAPP remained unchanged although qualitative improvements came in almost every dimension of the programme from the teaching materials to the training of teachers. Critical to the thinking behind the innovation was the idea that a largely agrarian economy needed its young people to become knowledgeable about what sustained their way of life, to develop attitudes and skills which would lead them to a better understanding of this core dimension of Swazi society and which would encourage them to see the practice of agriculture as a worthwhile and even profitable activity. The evaluations described above showed that these aims were largely achieved.

However, the evaluations analyzed were of their time. What remains is an investigation of any longer-term effects of the SAPP, introduced more than forty years ago. Further, it is important to identify the key factors which led to the relative success of SAPP, especially as an early memory of the team leading the innovation was of an ODA[53] senior adviser visiting Swaziland pronouncing that *School agriculture has never worked anywhere in Africa so it won't work here*.

- New Government policy favoured teaching of agriculture in school;
- Individuals such as Leonard Sithebe, as well as the Principal Secretary and the Minister, were very enthusiastic and supportive;
- There was a good spirit of cooperation between ministries;
- The introduction of a new subject into the school curriculum did not cause a problem of overcrowding;
- Schools with adequate cultivable space were selected;
- The small size of the country greatly facilitated administration.

---

[53] ODA (the Overseas Development Administration) was a forerunner of the UK's current Department for International Development (DfID).

CHAPTER FOURTEEN

Looking Ahead: Outcomes from the Summative Evaluation

This chapter provides some observations concerning the Swaziland experience with teaching and learning Agriculture in secondary schools. There are many criticisms which may be made. Have the deficiencies noted after the first six years been rectified? Have proposals for improvement been acted on? Have other problems arisen and been solved?

It is easy to criticize but not always easy to find alternative and improved ways of doing things. It is important to recognize inadequacies so that research may be carried out to find better methods. We shall examine some of the worst pitfalls which may prevent satisfactory achievement of the original objectives and these are examined below. These comments refer to Swaziland, but many of these problems are likely to be experienced in other countries in Africa and beyond.

The first problem is inherent in any Government structure which consists of Ministries and Departments. Rivalry and lack of cooperation and coordination seem to result from human nature. The problem with school agriculture is that schools are the responsibility of the Ministry of Education, and most Ministries of Education have little technical expertise in agriculture, and therefore have to draw upon expertise from the Ministry of Agriculture. They are fortunate indeed if they receive a sympathetic hearing from that Ministry, which often concerns itself mainly with technical matters rather than training. Swaziland was very fortunate because the Director of Agriculture appointed himself to the Schools Agriculture Panel, supported the SAPP fully, and encouraged his staff to do the same. Technical assistance was received from the Ministry, particularly the Research Station, as well as from the Uniswa Faculty of Agriculture. This level of cooperation continued over the years.

The second problem concerns subsequent opportunities for pupils who have undergone a school agriculture programme. Those who take a strongly vocational view of this programme complain that it may be a waste of time to provide agricultural knowledge and skills to pupils whose opportunity to go farming commercially is limited by a lack of land. Traditional tenure does not normally allow the allocation of land to school leavers. Even to those fortunate enough to have enlightened fathers who allocate land to their sons or daughters, the comparison of small scale traditional farming with the possibilities of white or blue collar jobs away from the land is not usually regarded as favourable. The pupils are aware of this and it takes a teacher of exceptional ability and dedication to persuade the students that agriculture is worthwhile and enjoyable, however true this may be. Two comments need to be made against this argument: first, to provide young people with agricultural skills and knowledge is a great deal better than not doing so; and secondly, the programme is not intended to be an exclusively vocational one, and has objectives broader than only to prepare individuals to become farmers! Once the purpose of teaching pupils about agriculture in secondary schools is better understood, it would be much better accepted.

The third problem is related to the previous one, and is concerned with the lack of finance for school leavers. This could be partially overcome if the Junior Certificate examination and even more so the School Certificate after Form Five, was recognized as an indication that the student who passes well is more likely to be a successful farmer, and could therefore be more creditworthy.

Fourthly, to make an acceptable study of agriculture expects a certain level of literacy and numeracy among students starting the programme. Many teachers have expressed the concern that the pupils arriving at school for Year One lack the basic skills required to make an intelligent study of agriculture. It is quite pointless teaching about off-take, fertilizer rates, profit and loss, dip concentrations and so on if the students have limited understanding of numbers. An inadequate level of literacy and numeracy may be attributed to many causes such as poor nutrition, long walks to get to school, ill health, rapidly changing teachers, lack of numeracy in the home and so on. But of course this really applies to all subjects, including language and mathematical studies, and does not apply in any special way to Agriculture.

Fifthly, another problem faced by school agriculture is one which pervades society at all levels, especially in the developing countries, but in reality throughout the world, and this is a lack of perseverance. The writer has coined the expression *'the threshold of abandonment'*. Too often pupils, teachers and even administrators try something once and if it doesn't succeed, they give up. For example, some of the laboratory/ workshop/store buildings are not used; the original filmstrip projectors were used by only a few teachers who persevered until they found ways of providing blackout and overcoming problems of small picture size. In farming, in teaching, indeed in life, this is not enough. Persistence is a personality attribute which is vitally important in development and without it almost nothing will be achieved. The problem is that the threshold of abandonment is extremely low, and it needs to be raised in order to achieve development and consequent improvement in the standard of living. This is an extremely difficult task, but the writer believes that it is largely a matter of confidence. If a pupil is confident in his or her own ability, then even if he or she fails at something the first or second time, he or she will still be prepared to carry on and try again. This is a vital need and is essential as part of pre-service and in-service training of agriculture teachers. This is not the place to elaborate on how this should be done, but the use of praise, the giving of responsibility, clarity in the giving of instructions so that pupils are able to carry them out easily and are thus encouraged about their own ability, and other similar techniques, will help to build up confidence. The building up of the confidence of the pupils is one of the most important responsibilities of the teacher.

Sixthly, the next problem may be summarized with the word 'status'. The writer believes that the original design of the workshop as a type of 'potting shed' with a mud floor, gaps between blocks instead of windows, no plaster, etc. was largely adequate. Nevertheless, it was decided to erect a much more elaborate and far more expensive building, partly because Agriculture would be held in low regard if the building was seen to be poor in appearance in comparison with the science laboratory! In other words, functionality and economics were regarded as subservient to status!

This issue of 'status' has been tackled in recent years by one introduction which could well be broadened. There is an annual competition for 'the Woman Farmer of the Year'. This provides the opportunity for conveying status upon the winners and could be widened to include, for example, dairy farmer, pig farmer, chicken farmer, maize farmer, vegetable farmer both women and men, and at regional as well as national level!! Achievement of a status and recognition of effort and ability is a great help in developing confidence, an essential attribute for the successful farmer.

The seventh serious problem is the lack of sufficient time. The training materials prepared were based on the assumption that six periods a week for three ten week terms would be available. Nevertheless, teachers constantly complained that there was too much material. Rather than leave out portions of the material to accommodate this problem, most teachers tended to resort to cutting out the practical work. This was a common solution to the problem, and was almost disastrous since it defeated many of the objectives of the entire programme: development of practical skills, as well as attitudes to practical activities. The solution to this problem lies in a series of actions: first, the teachers must understand that practical work is extremely important and that it should not be sacrificed in the interests of covering the syllabus. Secondly and **fundamentally,** they should be strengthened in their ability to teach in a mixed theory/practical way and not to think in terms of a separation between these two. Thirdly, the syllabus should be lightened, by the introduction of options and expectations of a lesser number of modules being completed.

The eighth challenge is an administrative one. During the first eight years of the project, there were no established posts in the Ministry of Education. The effect of this on staff morale is very negative since it appears to indicate that the Government is only half-hearted about the introduction of Agriculture into schools. However, at the time of writing, the number of schools has risen from the seven which started in 1973 to very nearly all schools, so there must clearly be a high level of commitment. The biggest problem is that it is not generally recognized that Agriculture in schools is not the same as teaching science, geography or languages. It needs properly trained teachers, buildings, equipment, and most particularly a support service from experienced highly competent coordinators/ inspectors who are available to assist the teachers with the very practical problems which they face. This book is intended to help interested parties recognize these needs. By 2018, the team included a Senior Inspector and a group of inspectors for agriculture in each of the four regions of the country.

The ninth challenge is the need for an examination system which truly reflects what we actually want to measure. The shortcomings of the examination system described above have to be tackled urgently. The role of the examiner and the moderator needs to be strengthened, partly by defining their role much more fully, and partly by rewarding them financially for their effort. The teachers need to have a clear idea about how to evaluate practical skill achievement, and to be trained to do this.

The final challenge is the need for a manual describing in detail the functions of the Inspectors; this would include a detailed system of evaluation of practical agricultural skills. This needs to be developed as a matter of urgency.

Summary

Many of the problems outlined above are those which were identified at the beginning of the project, and further identified at the initial evaluation of the project in other evaluations later:

- The importance of avoiding inter-departmental conflict;
- Problems of land allocation for young people;
- Capital availability for potential young farmers;
- Lack of adequate literacy and numeracy among pupils;
- The need to build up confidence at all levels to overcome a lack of perseverance;
- The importance of ensuring that the status of Agriculture, and therefore of agricultural training, should not dominate economic and functional considerations;
- The content of the programme should be adjusted to the time available for quality implementation;
- Government should confirm its commitment to the programme by allocation of adequate personnel and finance at an early stage;
- A system of examinations should be developed which is a true reflection of the level of achievement of the objectives of the programme by those pupils who have completed it. This system should include training of teachers, examiners and supervisors to promote its effective implementation;
- The development of a manual describing the functions and responsibilities of Inspectors is an important development; this should ensure that teachers would be guided to follow the guidelines much more closely than has been done in many cases.

A critical overview of the Schools Agriculture Pilot Project

This section considers the project in its totality based upon the original objectives, approach and outcome.

The overall objective was 'to encourage pupils to regard farming as an enjoyable and profitable way of life, when properly practiced; and to stimulate positive attitudes to development and conservation.' The evaluations carried out in the early phase showed that there was a significant change to 'enjoyable' and a very highly significant change to 'worthwhile'. However it has to be realized that in many schools, the teaching was carried out in a monotonous way and the practical activities were carried out badly or not at all. It is difficult to see how those pupils could be said to have achieved the objectives. These shortcomings can be best addressed by reducing the pressure of time and by intensive in-service training of the teachers. A revival and revision of the use of the Teachers' Guide is also necessary.

The reaction to an understanding of development and conservation resulted in very highly significant improvements, as shown in the analysis of the evaluations. It may reasonably be claimed that between 1973 and 1979, some 13 000 boys and girls have been made aware of the possibility of enjoyment and profit in farming; have become more receptive to the efforts of development agencies and have become more positive in efforts to conserve the environment. The extent to which these improvements have been brought about by the SAPP, as distinct from other influences, is impossible to estimate.

The 'approach' indicated the intention to teach about the underlying scientific principles of farming. The extent to which this has been achieved depends largely on the ability of the individual teacher. Business aspects of farming were illustrated in several of the modules and the extent to which this was achieved depended largely on whether the teacher followed the programme as devised, and since in many cases they did not do so, the achievement here has been rather little. The role of development agencies was well achieved, but the objective about improving an understanding of career opportunities was not spelt out in any of the modules and was rather little achieved.

When we come to the 'outcomes', we find aspects which are difficult to assess. Self-reliance, resourcefulness and problem-solving ability are very important developmental attributes and to a considerable extent depend upon confidence. The programme, if carried out as planned, is designed to give individual responsibility to pupils with the intention that self-reliance will be developed. Throughout the course, pupils are faced with challenges in order to develop resourcefulness and problem-solving ability. The extent to which they have achieved these attributes will become more apparent at a later stage

Whether pupils have acquired an attitude to modern farming in the use of scientific methods through illustration in the school garden or livestock units will probably only be apparent when they have the opportunity at a later stage in life to make real life decisions. For example, it is possible to compare results in the school garden, where scientific methods have been used, with other fields in the locality where recommendations have not been followed.

Pupils were expected to acquire practical agricultural and management skills. The programme set out in the teachers' handbook if carefully followed would enable pupils to acquire many skills such as record-keeping, marketing and calculation of costs and returns. However it was clear that several schools had not adhered to the programme as recommended with the result that pupils in those schools would not have been able to acquire these skills.

It is necessary to consider the specific shortcomings of the SAPP as recorded at this stage, that is, after forty years. First, the major deficiency noted by the TETOC team was an inadequate teaching method. Reading out of the textbook is not an acceptable method of teaching. This resulted in dull, mechanical lessons and passive, often bored, pupils. The TETOC team also drew attention to the amount of time spent on routine duties. Although routine is an inevitable part of husbandry, the fact that teachers had to spend time supervising routine livestock care meant that they had less time for lesson preparation. Another criticism made was that there was little attempt made to bridge the gap between subsistence and modern agriculture.

Other problems, which still need to be tackled 40 years later, were the lack of time to carry out the activities recommended; the inadequacy of the examination system, especially with regard to evaluating achievement of practical skills; the rejection of the work cards without sufficient trial; the lack of effort to make proper use of the workshop laboratories; insufficient time and effort devoted to in-service training, largely due the overburdening of the Coordinators.

The applicability of the principles used in Swaziland to other countries

The principles underlying the SAPP development in Swaziland were outlined in Chapter One. To what extent could these principles be applied to other countries who are considering the inclusion of Agriculture in the curriculum of secondary schools?

The first group of principles are administrative. The gradual approach to the introduction of school agriculture is probably necessary in most circumstances because lack of human and material resources prevents more than a few schools each year being equipped and staffed adequately. Careful school selection is necessary to increase the chances of success in the early years. Care has to be taken regarding the levels at which Agriculture should be taught – primary, junior secondary, high school? Once there is acceptance of the necessity to teach Agriculture in schools, there must be a commitment to allocate sufficient time in the timetable for it to be taught adequately. A decision has to be made as to whether Agriculture is to be a 'core' subject in the curriculum. Adequate arrangements have to be made to ensure that inputs are available in the quantities and at the times they are required. The importance of pre-service and in-service training of teachers cannot be over-stressed. Finally, it must be recognize that a supervisory structure to provide administrative, technical and, especially, pedagogical support to the teachers is developed. While one inspector may be adequate for a group of schools in other subjects, there will be a need for a stronger team to provide the necessary support in Agriculture.

The second group of principles relate to curriculum structure. The selection of topics to be included in the curriculum is crucial. It is better to limit the range of topics severely in order to ensure that what is included is done well. The modular approach to materials production worked well in Swaziland. The material within a module may be programmed so that full details are provided of a way to teach. Experience shows that when teachers do not stick to the programme much more firmly, the quality of learning deteriorates sharply. Experienced teachers may deviate from the recommended methods and in fact can contribute to curriculum development very richly as a result of their experience, but departure from the recommended methods can only be justified when it is replaced by another system equally good or better.

The third group of principles relate to content. Involvement of the teachers in curriculum development is highly recommended. Efforts should be made to encourage close relationships with other topics taught in the school curriculum so that maximum use may be made of agricultural examples in mathematics, geography, science and so on. The importance of local relevance cannot be overstressed, and this is why it is justified to produce teaching materials within the country wherever possible. The style of writing should be simple and attractive. Due emphasis should be given to the tripartite nature of agricultural studies: a science, a practice and a business.

The final group of principles relates to teaching methods. Class organization should encourage individual initiative as well as group cooperation. The programme should be prepared in such a way that the maximum flexibility is possible. A strong emphasis should be given to the use of audio visual aids though never as a substitute for the actual thing. There should be an emphasis on teaching in a practical way whenever possible. Why talk about chickens in the classroom when you have some of them running around outside? Finally, nothing is more important than ensuring that teachers have developed the basic pedagogical skills of question and answer, use of the black (or white) board, pupil participation, setting of tasks to be prepared for future lessons; lesson planning and scheme of work preparation, with which the layout in the teachers guides can provide a great deal of help to the teachers.

CHAPTER FIFTEEN

**Developments in the Operation of Modern Agriculture
by Mr. Elson Khoza, Current Senior Inspector**

Although a lot of changes have taken place in a wide variety of dimensions in the operation of the programme, its central objective remains the same, namely to transform the agricultural industry of Swaziland through changing the pupils' mindset about agriculture and empowering them with functional knowledge and skills on the subject. The changes that have occurred in the programme have been necessitated by the dynamic nature of agriculture and agricultural education. Changes in the environment and generation of new knowledge and skills by practitioners and researchers and technological developments have been the driving forces in the changes that have taken place and these are reflected in the textbooks published by Oxford University Press. Criticisms made by the evaluation teams in the initial stages have been taken into account so that the pressure of too many topics has been much reduced. The programme has not been responsive enough to the change drivers due to financial constraints, lack of personnel and other forms of support. Thus there is a lot of catching up to do. Most of the changes in the Modern Agriculture programme have been initiated by the Ministry of Education and Training, particularly the Agriculture Subject Panel, Curriculum Coordination Committee, National Curriculum Centre, and the Examinations Council of Swaziland. All of these bodies have been at the forefront or guiding forces in the change processes.

The rationale undergirding changes in the programme is that for cost-effective and sustainable transformation of the country's agriculture industry, there should be a credible schools agriculture programme which needs to be robustly operated and monitored or supervised by committed and motivated and relevantly qualified personnel in a conducive environment. This would help to guarantee that the country develops a vibrant agriculture industry that would be globally competitive. Availability of a well-educated, knowledgeable and skilled work force would stimulate substantial investment in the industry by both local and foreign investors as they will be assured of good returns from their investment.

Vision of the Schools Agriculture Department

Swaziland should have a world class schools agriculture programme staffed with suitably qualified and competent personnel capable of consistently delivering good quality results. This would be evidenced by the emergence of knowledgeable and skillful agriculturists to cover the entire value chain of the industry, that is, farmers, agriculture engineers, agriculture economists, soil scientists, researchers, processors of agriculture products and so on, thus ensuring a sustainable and comprehensive transformation of the country's agriculture industry.

Mission of the Schools Agriculture Department

The mission of School Agriculture is to train learners of high quality with the relevant knowledge and skills needed for them successfully to pursue chosen agriculture careers and lifelong learning in the subject so that they can sustainably contribute to food security and economic development in the country, while enjoying fulfilled lives.

Composition of the Schools Agriculture Programme

There are three separate areas of responsibility for the Agriculture section of the Ministry of Education: first, the Modern Agriculture subject offered at primary and junior and senior secondary levels; secondly, the pre-vocational agriculture subject offered at senior secondary level; and thirdly, the schools feeding scheme aimed at strengthening food security in schools. This book is concerned with the first of these responsibilities.

Approach to the teaching of the subject

This has remained the same since the initiation. Teachers are still expected to adhere to the practical approach and to ensure connection between practical and theory lessons. However, not separating practical lessons from theory lessons remains a challenge, thus practical projects are not sufficiently utilized as teaching aids in conducting the teaching and learning process in the subject. The greatly advocated school based assessment has also suffered a great blow due to deviation from this approach to learning. Hence the performance of pupils is variable in achievement depending upon the school and the teacher. This is principally due to lack of will, capacity and commitment among teachers and particularly due to inadequacy of training. Teachers need to be trained in how to conduct classes in a very practical way, using the suggestions laid out in the Teacher's Handbook, and also how to conduct practical assessment.

Revision of the Syllabus

Although the objectives of Modern Agriculture remain the same at all levels, the content, approach in delivering the syllabus content and assessment have been tweaked in numerous ways over the past 45 years. Revision and change of the syllabus has been made necessary by availability of new knowledge and skills concerning agricultural practices and the need to incorporate new enterprises into the curriculum, and to foster the much advocated practical approach in the teaching and learning process. In the past only one syllabus was used for both teaching and examination purposes for each level. Currently, we have a teaching syllabus and an examination syllabus for each level. Changes in the examination syllabus are normally initiated by The Examination Council of Swaziland. Changes in the examinations have been done to ensure comprehensive and objective measurement of pupils' performance at the end of each level, to put the country's schools external examinations on par with international standards, to make school based assessment grades more reliable and to ensure that examinations positively influence the teaching and learning process. To ensure comprehensive and objective assessment of pupils at the end of each level, both school based assessment and external examination grades are factored in when determining their final grades. On the basis of reports prepared by examiners and concerns voiced by agriculture teachers, it can be concluded that there is a lot of room for improvement in the preparation and processing of external examinations and school based assessment to ensure that they accurately reflect pupils' achievement. This indicates the strong need for capacity building in this facet of the curriculum.

Changes in Text Books

Significant changes have taken place in the text books used as teaching aids in offering the subject. For each class at the primary and junior secondary levels there is a textbook addressing the syllabus content to be covered by the pupils. The individual units used as an approach in producing textbooks was abandoned as it was found to be uneconomical. A wide range of new topics have been added to cater for changes in the syllabi at all levels. The most recent set of textbooks (2012, with further impression in 2018) produced by Oxford University Press is clear and well-illustrated, and considerably changed from the original ones produced in 1973!

Agriculture Subject Coordinator to Inspector

This name change was necessitated by the need to align the operational structure of the department with that of other subjects and changes in the nature of the work the programme supervisors were expected to perform. As quality assurers, they needed to execute more complex technical tasks in ensuring that teachers were competent enough to conduct the teaching and learning process and school based assessments. They were also responsible for assisting teachers to develop a conducive environment for the smooth and successful conduct of these activities. This included monitoring and moderating school-based assessment, ensuring adherence to government policies and regulations by school administrators and teachers, facilitating development of teaching and learning materials, assisting partners operating projects meant to enhance the environment within which the subject was being offered and the general school conditions and other duties. The change in the name has been accompanied by an increase in salary for the supervisors/inspectors.

In-service Training

A great deal of effort was being made in this regard and is being driven by the quest for continuous improvement in the performance of the programme. However, this area appears to be the weakest link in the operation of the programme. Underperforming schools and teachers are not getting enough assistance to enable them to make the expected transformation in their performance. This is attributable to lack of adequate support by stakeholders in terms of needed facilities/tools/ resources and lack of a systematic approach in executing this vital exercise. Development and equipping of a suitable institution and capacitating inspectors will go a long way to the realization of the fruits of in-service training in the programme.

Availability of Tools Required to Achieve Programme Objectives

Government is chiefly responsible for ensuring that all basic resources needed to attain the above are available. However, reinforcement of the government efforts by other stakeholders will go a long way towards cost-effective achievement of the programme's objectives. Areas where reinforcement is needed include: financing construction and equipping of infrastructure needed in schools, providing vehicles required by inspectors to conduct their duties, development of a subject in-service training centre[54], construction of suitable houses for the inspectors, continuous training of inspectors, development and supply of teaching aids and technological equipment needed in the operation of the programme and improvement of pre-service training programmes.

---

[54] This could include the use of the facilities available at the Faculty of Agriculture, Uneswa at Luyengo; as well as facilities developed for the training of primary teachers at the School Agriculture Centre, Ezulwini.

CHAPTER SIXTEEN

A Model for Agricultural Teacher Education
By Professor Comfort B.S. Mndebele

Introduction

One of the critical aspects in the teaching of agriculture in secondary schools in Swaziland was the competence of the teacher, and this necessitated a teacher preparation programme. Until 1973, the subject "Agricultural Science" was taught by teachers trained in the teaching of science, in particular Biological sciences. Teaching placed emphasis on the basic sciences with little emphasis on agriculture. Furthermore, the practical classes were almost entirely based on in-door laboratory experiments. Out-door experiential learning placing emphasis on raising crops and the husbandry of livestock was ignored. This was quite understandable, because the teachers were prepared to teach Biology and Physical Science, despite the fact that the subject was called "Agricultural Science". Thus Agricultural Science was taught by non-agriculture teachers, and they used science textbooks (Biology in particular). There was a need to change the name of the subject in line with the paradigm shift which placed emphasis on practical agriculture. The new name was "Modern Agriculture". The introduction of Modern Agriculture at the secondary level (Grades 8 to 10) came with a new approach. The framework adopted was three-pronged: teacher preparation/education, formal examination of the subject Modern Agriculture, and the production of locally relevant instructional materials (textbooks). Agricultural Science was taught by non-agriculture teachers, and they used science textbooks (Biology in particular). This Chapter describes the education/preparation of agriculture teachers for secondary schools. During the initial period which this book covers, most of the teachers were expatriates, but today (2018), almost all the teachers have been trained locally at the University of Eswatini.

Agricultural Education Centre Model

An Agricultural Education Centre (AEC) was established in the Faculty of Agriculture of the University. This was intended to be an example modelled on the secondary school setting, a prototype, in terms of building structures, ie. the agriculture classroom, livestock houses, and garden. A classroom with a toolshed attached to it was constructed. The classroom was identical to that found in the secondary schools offering Modern Agriculture. Two types of livestock reared in the school were included in the Modern Agriculture syllabus. These were broiler and layer chickens, raised in cages and also on deep litter to allow a study of comparison in terms of production and costs. The other livestock enterprise concerned rabbits. A further component of the Model was the garden to raise vegetables and also field crops. A small fish pond was established at the AEC even though some schools did not have a fish pond. Fish production was in the Junior Certificate syllabus and so it was important to have a fishpond in this demonstration area. Another enterprise introduced at the AEC was a small fruit tree orchard. Most schools could not afford this enterprise even though it was in the Junior Certificate syllabus. In short, the teacher education programme needed a small farm, and this would also be the ideal in a school.

Agriculture Teacher Education Programme

In the development of an agricultural teacher education programme in the Faculty of Agriculture, a holistic approach was adopted in which competence presupposes the individual qualities and attitudes of teachers, as well as their skills and knowledge resulting from experience. In the development of the pre-service agriculture teacher education programme, there was consideration of the challenges of our times, such as multicultural co-existence, the dominance of technology, the evolution of the sciences and the rapid renewal of knowledge. Schools aim at preparing students not only for the present, but for the ever-changing future. Therefore professional competence of teachers was defined as inclusive of: a) Personality traits, attitudes and beliefs; b) Pedagogical knowledge and skills including teaching methodology; c) Subject knowledge; d) Knowledge of learners; e) School curriculum knowledge, f) General pedagogical knowledge, and g) Knowledge of contexts (Liakopoulou, 2011).

Curriculum balance between Education and Agriculture

The pre-service agricultural education programme admits high school leavers with Grade 12 Cambridge School Leaving Certificate with high grades. Initially the University offered a two year then subsequently a three year Diploma in Agricultural Education, graduates of which would be certified to teach at the secondary school level, Grades 8 to 10. After the first few years, the Diploma programme was phased out and a four-year degree was introduced. In both the Diploma and Degree programmes, agriculture teacher education and agriculture subject matter courses were taught concurrently. At the end of the four years, agriculture student teachers graduate with both professional pedagogical courses and agriculture subject matter content. An eight-week's block of teaching practice was fitted into the four years. This is the Model or Framework adopted by the University.

The Agricultural Teacher Education curriculum is split with about 80% agriculture subject matter content and 20% professional-pedagogical courses. In the first Semester of Year one the students take basic sciences courses including Biology, Chemistry, Physics, and Mathematics. In the second Semester of Year One, students take the applied science courses including Botany, Zoology, Biochemistry and, Soil Chemistry which gradually introduce them to the agriculture subject matter curriculum. The 80% of the agriculture subject matter includes: a) Agricultural Bio-systems and Engineering; b) Animal Sciences; c) Agricultural Economics and Management; d) Crop Production; and e) Horticulture. The professional-pedagogical courses include: a) Educational Psychology; b) Teaching Methods and Testing in Agriculture; c) Education and Management; d) Curriculum Theory and Development; e) Foundations of Agricultural Education; f) Instructional Materials Design and Development; g) Teaching Practice.

Upon successful completion of the four year degree programme, the graduates are certified teachers with a professional qualification to teach both at the secondary (Grades 8 to 10) and high school (Grades 11 and 12) levels. They teach the whole spectrum of the Junior Certificate syllabus and the Overseas Cambridge Ordinary Level syllabus. It has been noted that there is now an oversupply of teachers of Agriculture at both secondary and high school levels. However, the preparation of these teachers is not geared towards teaching the Pre-Vocational Agriculture curriculum which is offered in Grades 11 and 12 parallel to Modern Agriculture. Preparation of teachers for the Pre-Vocational Agriculture syllabus was conducted once when the programme was getting ready for the launch. It was a one-off teacher education programme for selected teachers of agriculture who already possess training to teach Modern Agriculture.

Agriculture Teachers Teaching Mathematics and Science

In the recent past, teachers of agriculture have been requested to teach Mathematics and Science at secondary school level in the main, and high school level in selected cases. This has come about as a result of the increasing shortage of mathematics and science teachers. Agriculture teachers have a relatively strong academic background in the natural sciences (Maths, Physical Sciences, and Biology). Their strength is as a consequence of the entry requirement into the programme noted above. Furthermore, later in the degree programme, they take other applied science courses.

In some instances teachers of agriculture take positions of science teachers' right from initial appointment by the Teaching Service Commission (TSC). Research conducted in the teaching of sciences by agriculture teachers has confirmed that head teachers have a preference for agriculture teachers to include mathematics and science, particularly at the secondary school level.

In Edziwa and Chivheya (2012) knowledge in subject matter has been found to be an important characteristic of an effective teacher. The subject matter knowledge within agricultural education is complicated in that Agriculture, as a subject, encompasses a wide variety of disciplines. The agriculture teacher is expected to teach all areas of agriculture to include: Agricultural Economics, Agricultural Engineering, Animal Science, and Crop Science. Above all the role of the teacher of agriculture is to create an enthusiasm for and life-long commitment to agriculture as a dominant issue in the future of individual students and the communities from which they come. A central concern in the Modern Agriculture programme has always been the affective domain – how can positive attitudes towards agriculture be encouraged in school pupils and how can the teacher be prepared to carry out this important task? The degree programme at the University of Eswatini is an example of a successful approach to this challenge.

Reference:

Liakopoulou, M. (2011). The professional competence of teachers: Which qualities, attitudes, skills and knowledge contribute to a teacher's effectiveness? *International Journal of Humanities and Social Science, 1 (21) 66-78*

Edziwa, X. & Chivheya, R. (2012). Agriculture teacher education in Zimbabwe: A Teacher-Mentors' view of trainee teachers holding National Certificate in Agriculture. *Journal of Emerging Trends in Educational Research and Policy Studies*, 3(4), 495-500

CHAPTER SEVENTEEN

Living Forward and Understanding Backward: How the Swaziland Experience Fits with Today's World: Challenges Associated with the Introduction of Agricultural Education in Schools
By Dr. Robert Langley-Smith

The account of the rise and spread of 'Modern Agriculture' within the school system of Swaziland which has been described and analyzed in the preceding chapters provides a living exemplar of what can be achieved given certain building blocks are put in place and a sustainable structure established for continued success. It is clear from the history of attempts to increase the relevance of the school curriculum to the daily life of pupils and their communities that many of these essentials are frequently under-emphasized or missing altogether. Prominent among the causes of failure or limited success is the lack of clear aims for such programmes - are they meant to be pre-vocational, to link the school experience more closely to the local reality or to prepare pupils for a life of limited opportunity in a rural environment? This lack of clear aims is often an outcome from unclear policies from the Ministry of Education where white-collar employment remains the often unspoken and popular goal of formal education. Too often the big agencies like the World Bank have linked formal education too closely to modern-sector economic development, characterizing pupils purely in terms of their likely contribution to modern- sector economic growth.

Resistance from schools, parents, pupils and their communities has also been a major factor in the lack of success of curriculum diversity. Harking back to the 1960s, Patrick van Rensburg's 'Brigades' in Botswana set out, with full Government support, to vocationalize secondary education whilst academic education was retained in the mainstream schools. Parental resistance and pupil rejection of the model led to its gradual demise. Singer (2012) describes the early days of the movement when the charismatic van Rensburg was able to encourage students to build their own school, thus developing skills and expertise. Over time the gaps began to develop, especially when the building students found that they could not sustain their activities as supplies and equipment were expensive. The inability of communities to absorb numbers of bicycle repair-men, weavers and subsistence farmers was also a significant factor in the Brigade system's slow decline. The contrast with the approach taken in Swaziland is quite clear. Where Modern Agriculture presented itself as a well-resourced and supported programme integrated with the broader curriculum in Swaziland, van Rensburg's efforts represented a parallel system designed to address a specific perceived weakness in the school system – its lack of practical subjects in an environment where it appeared in the 1960s and 1970s that opportunities for modern sector work would be few. The discovery and exploitation of Botswana's immense mineral resources changed all that and a community-based subsistence working life no longer appealed to the youth of Botswana.

As the Swaziland experience demonstrated well there is a level of complexity in mounting a practical subject like Modern Agriculture which does not apply to more academic subjects. Although teachers may be trained, curriculum materials made available and poultry sheds, tools, fertilizers and other apparatus may be acquired by a Ministry, the personnel to train staff, to distribute materials and to monitor their use means a level of labour intensity missing from, say, the mounting of reforms to the teaching of mathematics or history. This dimension has frequently been under-estimated or under-funded.

The initial and recurrent costs of the equipment and other resources essential for a successful agriculture programme for schools have also presented a major barrier to success. One of the motivating factors in getting pupils 'on board' the new subject of Modern Agriculture was the obvious influx of interesting materials, tools and equipment, simple structures like poultry houses and the novelty of caring for livestock in school. All these things cost money and as, noted above, the donor community played an important role in ensuring the supply of the necessary tools and equipment.

The lack of trained staff at school and Ministry levels is another factor which inhibits successful development of complex curriculum reform. In most African countries this is true across the board. Competent teachers of mathematics and science are hard to find, partly because people with such skills can find better paid employment in the private sector. Training competent people for teaching and supervision often leads to leakage of such personnel, once again into the private sector. Making teaching and its ancillary roles attractive is a constant challenge even in developed economies.

A practical subject like Modern Agriculture also carried challenges with regard to supervision and monitoring of the programme in practice. Unlike other school subjects agriculture requires a great deal of professional and practical support. Materials have to be transported to school sites which are often hard to reach, transport and drivers have to be available and the financial burden of the provision of materials is often heavy for Ministries of Education.

Lack of suitable teaching and learning materials presents another problem. As noted above, ready-made textbooks, charts and posters may be available but may lack relevance to a specific environment. The preparation of workbooks, work cards and other materials demands skilled input from professional curriculum people who not only know their subject but also understand the pupils and their communities. A whole literature has been developed around the concept of 'Indigenous Knowledge'[55] and much research has been conducted in Africa and elsewhere on bridging the gap between western epistemology and the ways of knowing and understanding embraced in more traditional societies. That Modern Agriculture in Swaziland managed to do this is a tribute to the way in which the curriculum was developed with much input from the classroom practitioners.

Overcrowded curricula leaving no space for agriculture present another challenge. The focus in African schools on the academic rather than the practical is a well-known phenomenon. For years after independence Zambian schools were still offering 'British Constitution' as an examination subject. A significant inheritance from colonial days for many African school systems was the belief that only the academic and examinable subjects like English, History, Chemistry and Mathematics were worth studying. Allied to this 'habitus' was parental resistance to subjects which could be 'taught at home'. Attempts in Botswana, Lesotho and Swaziland to introduce a school subject called 'Development Studies' were designed to combat the elitism seen to arise from focusing on purely academic subjects. It should also be pointed out that Modern Agriculture was introduced at a time when Swaziland was inundated with curriculum innovation sponsored by various donors such as Sweden and UNDP. The primary school curriculum was also being completely redesigned

---

[55] See Breidlid A (2013) *Education, Indigenous Knowledges and Development in the Global South*, London, Routledge

by a USAID team so the curriculum environment was a turbulent one during the introduction and development of Modern Agriculture as a subject.

Given this catalogue of potential and actual pitfalls it is worth revisiting the conditions which led to the success of Swaziland's curriculum innovation.

How Swaziland's Modern Agriculture Programme overcame these barriers.

Research into educational change and reform, including implementation of new curricula is widely recorded. Perhaps the key figure in the field of change theory in education is Michael Fullan of the Ontario Institute for Studies in Education. His work on reform in education is seminal and has had far-reaching influence within the economically advanced world and in the South. To summarize briefly his principles for sustainable change would not do justice to the complexity of the processes Fullan describes and analyzes. However, the box below attempts to do this as an aid to understanding how Swaziland's programme worked and what those wishing to replicate a successful programme should think about and design their innovations accordingly.

Fullan's Principles for Successful Change in Education
(Fullan, 4th Edtn.,2007)

- Change aimed at bridging the gap between pupils who perform well and those who do less well
- Stick to the basics (of literacy, numeracy and well-being)
- Tap into people's dignity and respect
- Get the best people working on the challenge
- Change by doing rather than planning – be socially based and action oriented
- Recognise lack of capacity and work continually to improve it
- Ensure continuity of good leadership
- Build internal accountability linked to external accountability
- Develop conditions for positive pressure to succeed
- Build public confidence

Like all such check-lists, not all are equally reflected in any given programme but it is already clear how Swaziland's Modern Agriculture Programme conformed to these principles. In a nutshell the Modern Agriculture innovation was characterized by –

- Champions identified and active – Ministry of Education (MoE),
- University, donors and Individuals;
- Leadership shared and sustained over time; team building embraced as an important principle;
- Clear aims – modern, business-like, interesting course of study which respected the role of agriculture in the national economy and culture;
- Policy embraced by schools/communities who were consulted in advance;
- Careful initial selection of schools/staff;
- Curriculum design answered perceived needs/priorities;
- Locally developed materials;
- Curriculum space freed up;
- Training set up at all levels: teachers, supervisors, university staff;
- Costs shared by donors; MoE took ownership over time.

However, a further theoretical concept which throws light on Swaziland's success is Elmore's theory of 'Backward Mapping' (Elmore, 1979). In essence Elmore argues that reformers usually start at the top to persuade practitioners to adopt a new approach or the Minister returns from an international conference and immediately summons his or her professional staff and instructs them in the latest UN policy directive, hoping for transformational implementation to follow – forward mapping or planning. Elmore argues from the opposite standpoint. Backward Mapping requires going to the grass roots, the lowest level of implementation to pose the question, 'If the Ministry were to introduce a certain innovation or change, what problems would it create for you and what opportunities would arise from the change?' In the light of the findings a much more realistic programme can be developed, rooted in the day-to-day practice already in existence. A recent Norwegian initiative in South African higher education illustrates this principle in terms of building on existing practices, extending and refining them rather than imposing a new model. Further reference will be made to principles emerging from that project[56] but suffice it to say that Modern Agriculture as a programme was

[56] See *Driving Change,* (2014) Ed. Trish Gibbon, African Minds, Somerset West, South Africa

firmly rooted in 'Backward Mapping' through which teachers, education officers, communities and ministry officials were all included in the design and implementation of the innovation.

How does the Swaziland experience compare with international trends?

Since the introduction of Modern Agriculture in the Swaziland of the 1970s there have been significant changes in our views of the economics of development. These views have been much influenced by a parallel change in our understanding of the global environment. Such initiatives as the Millennium Development Goals (MDGs) and their successors, the Sustainable Development Goals (SDGs), have created a much more integrated and holistic view of what development might and should mean. Although the Millennium Development Goals failed to materialize fully by their deadline date of 2015, much progress had been made, particularly in terms of health and education benefits for the poorest. The Sustainable Development Goals, more complex, wide-ranging and integrated, raise their own specific problems in that they are based on a controversial economic model of further exploitation of natural resources, further consumption and a wider spread of consumerism leading to growth. The notion of prosperity without growth (Jackson, 2009) has yet to be embraced by the global players like the World Bank, despite an estimate by 'The Spectator' that the Sustainable Development Goals will take 207 years to achieve, will take trillions of dollars and that world economic growth would have to increase by a factor of 175 if the elimination of poverty is to be achieved within the given time frame.

Despite the obvious faults of MDGs and SDGs they do illustrate an attempt to situate national development within a global perspective. Thus the mounting of a curricular programme to address a significant gap in the education of rural children is more often seen today within such a perspective. It is no longer seen as a local or even national issue but as a survival mechanism that will contribute massively to food security and broader community development among the poorest people of the South. This is not to say that technological advances will pass by the rural poor but that a realistic view of development reveals that, say, the nomadic people of Chad are unlikely to find their future prosperity in high tech factories. Much more likely that they, and people like them throughout Africa, will benefit from self-reliance and self-employment which usually means agriculture in one form or another. Our view of development, although still dominated by the capitalist/consumerist mind-set, has at least moved towards a more integrated and ecologically-based model.

Evidence from the field: some case studies

Comparing Swaziland's experience from the 1970s and 1980s with current thinking and practice leads to further analysis of the dominant theoretical and conceptual dimensions of thinking about education over this period. Knobloch et al (2007) writing about the benefits of teaching and learning about agriculture in the United States, note that integrating agriculture into school curricula brings learning to life through experiential learning, a community-based curriculum and the opportunity to apply learning in real-life situations. Schools can play an important role in getting general health messages across in an authentic way. Knobloch also indicates that teachers have noted links between students' understanding of food production and developing a respect for nutrition, and more broadly, agriculture's role in society and the environment.

Theories of integration underpin the teaching of agricultural topics across the curriculum. Students then discover the 'big picture' and gain greater insight into other content areas. The research of Knobloch et al indicates that contextualizing the teaching of agriculture is all-important. Topics such as conservation, the environment, food production, plants and seed development, insects, animals, agricultural careers, the cycles of life and nature, food and nutrition were listed by students as most important. Instructional resources were noted as problematic unless special efforts were made. Few teachers had access to good materials. Curricular modules and lesson plans were most in demand plus ideas of projects and activities to be pursued. Integrating agriculture into the curriculum brought about connectedness and authenticity for many teachers.

Three major themes emerged from the work of this team: connectedness, situatedness and authenticity. Connectedness refers to the extent to which knowledge of agriculture helped pupils understand the relationship between humans, their food and their environment. Situatedness refers to locating studies in the grade and level of the pupils, and authenticity to the opportunities for pupils to see how agriculture was connected to real-life experiences through the hands-on, experiential approach adopted across the curriculum.

Turning to work in Zimbabwe, Majoni (2016) notes that attempts to introduce agriculture into the school curriculum date back to the 1950s although the later Lewis Taylor Report of the 1970s recommended the dropping of agriculture per se as there was a shortage of land and of teachers and a history of failure to make the subject work. In 1982 Environmental and Agricultural Science was introduced with the objective of making pupils aware of the relationship between the physical, biological and human aspects of the environment, fostering a positive interest and appreciation of a well-managed environment and the development of basic skills and concepts in agricultural practices. However, schools did not have qualified staff, equipment, laboratories or land available. Majoni's research revealed that this lack of basic resources, duplication of topics within science and agriculture, lack of land and no financial support from Government doomed the whole enterprise to failure.

The work of Kabugi (2014) in Kenya reveals similar issues and problems. This study aimed to explore institutional and non-institutional challenges to teaching agriculture in the secondary schools of a selected district. Although all schools in the district offered agriculture few students opted for the subject, preferring Business Studies with which it was paired in the curriculum. A high proportion of students who did choose agriculture stated that they would consider a career in agriculture. Once again, lack of land, lack of tools and equipment and poor classroom facilities hindered teaching and learning. School punishment regimes such as weeding gardens provided a further disincentive. Teacher workload was another barrier to success and external conditions such as rainfall patterns and suitable soils also militated against agriculture as a school subject.

> **From the Jamaica Observer of July 18th 2015**
>
> Janet Hylton, Chair of Generation 2000, writes that there is a need to re-examine agricultural education for a successful future. People believe that teaching science and business skills will provide the food and environment changes the world needs. Agricultural education will need to change although its methods can be enjoyable for pupils. High quality teachers and strong state and sectoral leadership will be necessary for success – agricultural literacy will be an important goal. Agricultural education must be integrated with all other subjects and community-based programmes must use local expertise to ensure full support for the work in schools. A refined vision is needed nationally focusing on the production of food security and on career preparation.

Madagascar's 'Pro Vert' curriculum provides yet another example of an integrated attempt to 'make schools greener' by building a curricular approach around key issues in conservation and agriculture. This programme of the Lutheran Church of Madagascar (LFM) was designed as a bridgehead from which the whole national school curriculum could eventually learn[57]. Of particular interest were the locally produced materials in Malagasy, the linkages between schools and neighbouring agricultural colleges and a supervisory team somewhat akin to the Swaziland model laid out in earlier chapters. Schools were encouraged to develop tree nurseries to help in re-afforestation and there was strong integration of schools with their communities, the situatedness and contextualization referred to earlier. Harber (2014) describes the Pro Vert programme as consisting of environmental, educational and social activities designed to mainstream the planting of trees and vegetables, training in handicrafts, environmental protection, health-related activities and practical skills. The Project Document notes that: *The Green Education programme*

---

[57] See also Smith R.L. *'Who owns the curriculum? Governments, NGOs and the learning needs of African pupils'*, Journal of Curriculum Studies, March 2007, Vol 2, No.2, pp 1 - 17

attempts to reconcile education and the environment and by this means to contribute to sustainable development'. As well as its environmental focus the Pro Vert programme was designed to address issues of gender equality, inclusion and pedagogic reform. As a bridgehead initiative Pro Vert was intended to provide lessons from experience for the broader school curriculum in Madagascar, the expectation being that it would move from project status to the mainstream. Unfortunately, Norwegian funding which had been critical for the establishment of the programme, came to an end and the longer term sustainability of Pro Vert remains problematic. Like so many similar innovations, its principles and structure remain sound but the critical element of external support cannot be expected to sustain a programme indefinitely.

Of less immediate application but still relevant is the growing number of Accelerated Learning Programmes (ALP), particularly in Asia and West Africa (Longden, 2013). ALPs are designed to provide an alternative to the mainstream school which is either inaccessible to village children or where they have previously failed. The notions of contextualization and situatedness are strongly represented in such programmes and although they offer a truncated version of the regular curriculum they cover sufficient material for successful pupils to be reintegrated into mainstream classes once they have completed the ALP. The use of local personnel as teachers, bonding the curriculum to rural realities and using practical learning with frequent supervisory visits ensures that the majority of pupils going through the accelerated programme are retained in school.

International perspectives at the macro level

Atchoarena and Gasperini (2003) in 'Education for Rural Development' note that efforts to relate schools to the rural environment are now a global phenomenon. Using the pupils' environment to enhance learning is now a key concept, not just in rural areas, although the report of a UNESCO/FAO workshop on these issues was primarily aimed at the rural child. Atchoarena and Gasperini's publication points out that theories of experiential learning (Kolb, 1981), theories of multiple intelligences (Gardner, 1999), socio-ecological models of the child's world (Moore and Young, 1978) and developmental psychology all add strength to an emerging model of experiential and contextualized learning and teaching. For such a model to succeed the three distinct elements of the home, the community and the school need to be linked effectively. Within the school efforts must be made to link work in agriculture or gardening with core subjects like science and language. Once again concepts like contextualization figure largely in the work of IIEP[58] and FAO (Atchoarena and Gasperini 2003). The discussion in 'Education for Rural Development' follows the familiar pattern of pleas for flexible guidelines for teachers, appropriate training and material support, use of innovative ways of teaching, the involvement of community members in the work of the school, the building of partnerships and, most significantly of all, the institutionalization of innovation rather than relying on bridgeheads or islands of change. Atchoarena and Gasperini conclude their analysis by pointing out that there is no universal model of agricultural learning; each culture or community must design a plan that addresses the needs of its own learners and educators.

Agricultural Education and Training (AET), Technical and Vocational Education and Training (TVET) and School Education

Perhaps the most significant macro-level development in the field of agricultural education has been the rise of AET and TVET as major players in addressing the ecological, environmental and food security issues confronting the Global South in particular. For too long agricultural education in its many forms has been the poor relation of formal, academic schooling and has been associated with failure to achieve in the mainstream school or as a second class form of further education. A detailed analysis of developments in AET and TVET would fall outside the present discussion[59] but these concepts represent a shift in thinking within the development community. Such concepts are deeply embedded in the current economic debate over the whole issue of development and what it should mean. Mention has been made above of ideas such as prosperity without growth and the controversial nature of the so-called Sustainable Development Goals. However, education's role in development is not a binary issue of schooling versus training. If Swaziland's Modern Agriculture innovation had as a central aim the relating of schooling to

---

[58] IIEP - the International Institute for Educational Planning (of UNESCO, Paris)

[59] See for example Wallace I and Nilsson E (Sept. 1997), Natural Resource Perspectives, London, ODI

community realities it provides a preview of such recent innovations as Norway's Pre and Post Primary Education Fund (2006 -12). This Trust Fund was set up within the World Bank with the aim of assisting countries in the constructing of plans for diversifying what is offered in the formal school sector. Typical of the Fund's activities was the assessment of skill demands in labour markets, promotion of public debates on existing capacity and reforms necessary, diagnostic work in specific sub-sectors, dissemination of knowledge at regional and national levels and the production of a number of significant policy publications. This brief description serves to illustrate the shift in attitudes towards skills education as part of the formal school curriculum. The 'big players' in education like the UN agencies and the World Bank are more engaged today in such developments, using their technical strengths to support change and provide the analytic and policy-related building blocks that individual countries need if they are to adapt their school systems to the development realities confronting them. Modern Agriculture in Swaziland was introduced as a means of contextualizing, and situating an authentic approach to schooling. The demand for this throughout the Global South has not diminished and, given the more ecologically conscious world view largely embraced at the macro-level of development practitioners and the greater awareness of communities and individuals of the finite nature of the planet's resources, exemplars like Swaziland's Modern Agriculture curriculum provide concrete evidence of what works and how it can be managed. The account of the establishment of SAPP in Swaziland (Eswatini) which this publication analyzes and presents offers not only a narrative of a success story but provides clear signposts for those still wrestling with the vexed question of how to make schooling relevant to pupils and communities both in the here and now but also for an unpredictable future.

References:

Atchoarena D and Gasperini L (2003) Education for Rural Development: Towards New Policy Responses, Paris, IIEP/FAO.

Breidlid A (2013) Education, Indigenous Knowledges and Development in the Global South, London, Routledge.

Elmore R F (1979) *Backward Mapping: Implementation Research and Policy Decisions*, Political Science Quarterly, Vol 94, No. 4.

Fullan M (2007) The new meaning of educational change (4th Edtn.) Routledge, Abingdon.

Gardner H (1999) Multiple Intelligences, New York, Basic Books.

Harber C (2014) Education and International Development: theory, practice and issues, Oxford, Symposium Books.

Jackson T (2009) Prosperity without Growth, London, Earthscan.

Kabugi S (2014) *Challenges to Teaching and Learning of Agriculture in Secondary Schools in Machakos County, Kenya,* http://ir-library.ku.ac.ke.

Knobloch N, Ball A and Allen C (2007) *The Benefits of Teaching and Learning about Agriculture in Elementary and Junior High Schools,* Journal of Agricultural Education, Vol 48, No. 3.

Kolb D (1981) Experience, Learning and Development; the Theory of Experiential Learning, Englewood Cliffs N.J., Prentice Hall.

Longden, K (2013) *Accelerated Learning Programmes: What can we learn from them about curriculum reform?* EFA Global Monitoring Report 2013/2014, UNESCO, Paris.

Majoni C (2016*) Introducing Agriculture as a Subject in the Primary School Curriculum in Zimbabwe,* International Journal of Information Research and Review, Vol 3, pp 1669-1671

Moore R and Young D (1978) Children and the Environment, New York, Plenum.

Singer R (2012) *'I'll* teach you to build a school' Front Porch Review, Vol 4, April 2012. (www.frontporchrvw.com).

World Bank *Report of a Review of the Norwegian Pre- and Post-Primary Education Fund, 2006 -12,* Washington D.C, World Bank.

29638562R00090

Printed in Great Britain
by Amazon